THINKING & REASONING, 2004, *10* (2), 113–121

Introduction: Why is understanding the development of reasoning important?

Henry Markovits
University of Plymouth, UK

Pierre Barrouillet
University of Bourgogne, France

This special issue of *Thinking & Reasoning* focuses on the development of reasoning, with contributions from several distinguished developmental researchers. Although there is a long tradition of developmental work on reasoning, there has been a marked decrease in such studies recently. Both this fact and the reasons for it constitute the rationale for this special issue. Much of the initial impetus for research about reasoning was motivated by Piaget's theory of formal operations (Inhelder & Piaget, 1958). Piaget considered that an understanding of the formal rules of inference was the epistemological basis for the kind of hypothetico-deductive mode of thinking that appears in adolescence. This led to an explosion of research focused on two (somewhat mistaken) predictions that were made from this theory, which have generally led to the present decline of both Piagetian theory and developmental research on reasoning. The first was the prediction that young children who do not possess the basic competence for formal operations (or in some cases, such as conservation and transitivity, concrete operations) will be unable to give the right answer to any problem that can be identified as concrete or formal operational. A series of studies in a variety of domains (Bryant & Trabasso, 1971; Dias & Harris, 1988; Hawkins, Pea, Glick, & Scribner, 1984) showed that very young children can respond "correctly" to many such problems. In fact, this basic analysis has been extended to babies (e.g., Baillargeon & DeVos, 1991) and other species such as pigeons (Von Fersen, Wynne, Delius, & Staddon, 1991). This led to claims that very young children are "logical" and that the basic competencies that Piaget identified as taking many years to develop

---

Correspondence should be addressed to Professor Henry Markovits, Centre for Thinking and Reasoning, Department of Psychology, University of Plymouth, Devon PL4 8AA, UK. Email: henry.markovits@plymouth.ac.uk

---

© 2004 Psychology Press Ltd
http://www.tandf.co.uk/journals/pp/13546783.html   DOI: 10.1080/13546780442000006

appear to be present very early, if they are not essentially innate, something that is clearly suggested by studies with babies and pigeons. The basic conclusion of these studies is that the most interesting problems in psychology consist of documenting the nature and basis of early competence. Development is seen as uninteresting, since it essentially involves problems of implementation or detailing performance factors that make this more or less difficult.

The second general prediction that was made from Piaget's theory led researchers in a completely different direction. This was that formal operational competence must inevitably develop and that any educated adult should be capable of giving the correct answer to any and all problems that can be identified as formal operational. This led to studies which clearly showed that, in many cases, adult reasoners do not give the logically appropriate response to a variety of reasoning problems (e.g., Wason, 1968). This in turn prompted a general claim that formal operational competence is not a useful concept since few reasoners appear to have it in a consistent way. This line of research has also led to a decline in development work, since there is no point in looking at the development of something that is not present.

Thus, on the one hand, many researchers claim that logical competence (as defined by Piaget's theory) is innate or close to it, while, on the other hand, other researchers claim that logical competence (as defined by Piaget's theory) is not present even in adults. As a result of these two wildly divergent conclusions, and therefore for very contradictory reasons, research whose aim is to trace the development of reasoning has become relatively rare. One of the most direct consequences of this is that many theories have little or no explicit developmental components, leaving the question of what, if anything, happens between birth and adulthood essentially unanswered. Another consequence is the clear fragmentation that exists between studies that look at children's reasoning and those that look at adult reasoning. This has allowed researchers who study children and those who study adults to make claims that may well be in direct or implicit contradiction to existing empirical evidence. For example, some researchers (Hawkins et al., 1984; Leevers & Harris, 1999) have claimed that very young children are able to reason logically with abstract or false premises. However, claims of early competence must also explain why this kind of reasoning is difficult even for educated adults (e.g., George, 1997), something that is simply ignored. Another example is that of Johnson-Laird's mental model theory. While paying relatively little attention to development, the theory's claim that the major constraint in reasoning is working memory capacity allows some clear predictions about younger children. Specifically, children should invariably show conditional reasoning patterns corresponding to an interpretation of the conditional that is either "and" or the biconditional (Johnson-Laird &

Byrne, 2002). However, research on children's reasoning has shown that this is simply not true (e.g., Kuhn, 1977; Markovits, Venet, Janveau-Brennan, Malfait, Pion, & Vadeboncoeur, 1996; Rumain, Connell, & Braine, 1983). In both cases, these theories are able to make unconvincing claims since the relatively hermetic nature of research on children and that on adults allows researchers to ignore a large quantity of empirical data.

If we leave aside, for the moment, the question of interpretation, the two research programmes that we have spoken of can be summarised by two sets of results. One set comprises studies which have found that young children can reliably produce "correct" answers to some reasoning problems. The other set comprises studies which have found that adults do not reliably produce "correct" answers to other reasoning problems. Now, there is no reason to doubt either of these sets of results in themselves. The real question is just how to interpret them. At least one of the reasons that researchers looking at children's competence and those looking at adults' incompetence can arrive at what appear to be completely contradictory conclusions in what is nominally the same discipline, is that they rarely interact. This lack of interaction allows use of the same terms to describe what appear to be very different measures, and allows theories to simply ignore data that contradict some basic premises. We would argue that the clearest form of interaction is the developmental study, since (1) it presupposes some degree of continuity between children and adults, (2) it requires the use of compatible measures of a given concept across ages, and (3) it explicitly requires theoretical models to make clear predictions about the extreme points of development and the underlying mechanisms that explain change or lack of it.

The papers in this special issue of *Thinking & Reasoning* illustrate this point by examining development in three major contexts. The first relies on the basic idea that some critical changes during development are due to changes in reasoners' information processing capacities. Thus, Halford and Andrews present their model of relational complexity and attempt to model how this basic processing capacity could determine developmental patterns across several domains. The second context examines development in the light of current dual-process theories. These theories postulate the existence of two distinct systems of reasoning, one being associative and immediate, if not unconscious, and the other being rule-governed and effortful. While such theories provide the potential for interpreting at least some of the observed variability in reasoning as being due to the interplay between the two systems, they remain, at least for the moment, focused only on adult reasoning. They thus leave unanswered the same key questions as other current theories of reasoning, and a developmental approach, as suggested by papers from Klaczynski and Cottrell, or Handley, Capon, Beveridge, Denis, and Evans in this issue, is equally critical to understanding the nature of these theories. Finally, the third context postulates that at least some of the important differences observed in children's and adults' reasoning can be accounted for by metacognitive understanding and control. Papers by Kuhn, Katz, and Dean, and Moshman in this issue claim that one of the key developmental differences between children and adults, and often between reasoners of the same age but of differing ability, is the capacity to reflect on one's own reasoning, and to use the product of this reflection to organise complex reasoning processes.

INFORMATION PROCESSING CONSTRAINTS ON DEVELOPMENT

Information processing theories usually account for cognitive development by assuming that there is an age-related increase in computational power, which is often conceived of as an increase in cognitive, or working memory, capacity (Pascual-Leone, 1970; Case, 1985, 1992). Both the increase of this basic processing capacity and the increase of the knowledge base through learning would allow children to solve increasingly complex reasoning problems with age. Complexity is a function of the number of processing steps and the quantity of representations to be constructed, maintained, and manipulated. This kind of approach does not deny that young children might be able to perform optimally, even from a normative point of view, when the problems are simple and do not exceed their limited capacities or when relevant knowledge is readily available from long-term memory. The hypothesis of computational limitations can be used to account for the discrepancies observed in adults between actual responses and normative models. These would arise from performance errors in particularly demanding tasks with unfamiliar and decontextualised contents. We have recently put forward such a developmental theory for conditional reasoning by mental models, in which reasoning is constrained by both a limitation in working memory capacities and the efficiency of the retrieval process (Markovits & Barrouillet, 2002). Basically, the development of conditional reasoning would result from an increasing capacity with age to construct, maintain, and process a larger number of mental models in working memory. In the present special issue, Handley et al. provide evidence that working memory capacity in children is a good predictor of logical reasoning performance in conditional and relational problems when they involve belief neutral and knowledge-free contents (see also Barrouillet & Lecas, 1999, for similar findings in children, and Markovits & Doyon, in press, with adults).

In their Relational Complexity (RC) theory, Halford, Wilson, and Phillips (1998) go further by assuming that the complexity of reasoning is not a function of the total information to be processed in the task, but the number of independent variables that can be related in a single cognitive representation. Thus the difficulty of a given form of reasoning would depend on the relational complexity of the mental model required to represent the concept it involves. Because relations with more arguments have a higher computational cost, the complexity of relations and children's increasing processing capacity interact to determine developmental patterns of reasoning. In this special issue, Halford and Andrews suggest that children's reasoning can no longer be assessed by reference to the norms of logical inference, but by the complexity of the mental model needed to solve a specific task. For example, they argue convincingly that young children's success in making transitive inferences on the task used by Pears and Bryant (1990) is due to the specific requirements of this task, which can be solved with binary relational representations; whereas more traditional transitive inferences are ternary relational and thus appear later in development (after 5 years of age). In the same way, the complexity analysis applied to categorical syllogisms makes it clear that the most difficult of these problems involve a five-dimension representation, and thus are often failed even by adults who can only process quaternary relations. The authors conclude from their investigation of a large range of deductive reasoning domains that, though there are some experimental results indicating that children can occasionally perform well on tasks which seem to perplex adults (Klaczynski & Cottrell, this issue), the inferences of younger children are invariably less complex than those of older children.

The information processing approach is a valuable tool in modelling some basic developmental trends. It is less clear that this approach can, by itself, successfully account for variability in adult performance. It has been argued that the computational limitations hypothesis cannot totally explain the gap that exists between adult performance and the norms prescribed by formal logic (Stanovich & West, 2000). It has thus been assumed that some responses are not underpinned by an analytic and logically driven system of thought but by a more conversational and social system which is more associative and heuristic than rule-based. Thus, two reasoning systems, both being rational in some way, could coexist. The developmental implications of this dual process approach have not been worked out, but this theoretical framework could provide a fruitful avenue of research.

DUAL PROCESS ACCOUNTS

This contrast between two coexisting and distinct systems of reasoning has been described either as heuristic vs analytic (Evans, 1989), associative vs rule-based (Sloman, 1996), or tacit vs explicit (Evans & Over, 1996). These oppositions seem to refer to the more general one posited by Reber (1993) between implicit and explicit cognition. The first system, referred to as

System 1 by Stanovich and West (2000), encompasses automatic, largely unconscious, and undemanding processes that are part of an interactional intelligence involved in highly contextualised, socialised, and personalised situations. By contrast, the second system, System 2, encompasses controlled and demanding processes involved in analytic and logical intelligence required to deal with decontextualised situations. Because System 1 processes are automatic and largely unconscious, System 1 is primary, and the tendency to code specific features of problem content and to retrieve semantically associated information would constitute a fundamental computational bias. Thus, Stanovich and West (2000) suggest considering the logically driven System 2 as an override system for some of the automatic and obligatory computational results provided by System 1. The interplay between the two systems thus accounts for both young children's competence, which often occurs in highly contextualised and socialised problems where both systems cue the same response (Harris & Nunez, 1996), and adults' incompetence, which is mainly observed when the two systems cue different responses, as in the problems often used in the heuristic and biases literature.

At a first glance, dual process theories leave little room for development. Indeed, the processes involved in implicit cognition (System 1) are known to be largely independent of developmental or individual differences (Reber, 1993; Saffran, Aslin, & Newport, 1996; Vinter & Detable, 2003; Vinter & Perruchet, 2000). However, development could occur because the capacity to inhibit System 1 when System 2 and decontextualised reasoning is needed could increase with age. For example, Braine and O'Brien (1991) suggested that the development of the understanding of conditional sentences would be based on an increasing age-related capacity to set aside the pragmatic principles in situations that require logical treatment (e.g., laboratory tasks). In the present issue, Handley et al. provide evidence that the executive ability to inhibit heuristically cued responses based on prior beliefs plays a key role in the children's ability to decontextualise their reasoning (see also Simoneau & Markovits, 2003). In their contribution on children's understanding of sunk cost, Klaczynski and Cottrell suggest a slightly different hypothesis. The increased tendency of adolescents to set aside heuristics and make normative decisions could result from their greater willingness to engage in what they call "metacognitive intercession". The process of overriding implicit heuristic cognition is conscious and thus likely requires metacognitive abilities that develop with age. Interestingly, Klaczynski and Cottrell envision two other sources of development. First, inhibitory capacities and metacognitive abilities are not sufficient without the dispositional tendencies to use these capacities and abilities. Disposition against premature closure, cognitive confidence, or reflectivity are factors that could develop with age and account for at least a part of developmental differences in the same way they account for individual differences in using System 2 reasoning (Stanovich & West, 1997, 1998). Second, Klaczynski and Cottrell note that adults possess more analytic competence than children—something that is clear from information processing studies—but also more experiential knowledge and heuristics that are probably easier to activate with age. This last developmental trend, though usually overlooked, could be of particular interest if we suppose that the two systems of reasoning are optimised for different situations (contextualised or abstract) and different goals.

We have seen that metacognition plays, according to Klaczynski and Cottrell, a major role in the interplay between experiential and analytic processes. Many authors have suggested that metacognitive processes are in fact central to understanding the nature of cognitive development and the development of rational thought.

METALOGICAL DEVELOPMENT

Metacognition refers both to the ability to think about thinking, and to explicitly control the organisation of one's reasoning processes. The study of the development of metacognitive abilities has a long history. Metacognition as executive control has often been used to explain some basic competence–performance distinctions, specifically the all-too-common cases of children and adults who are able to solve problems in one context, but appear to be unable to do so in a different context. It also has been used as a label for the ability to create abstract concepts that are derived, not simply from empirical knowledge, but from some process of reflection upon the way that we think. As both Kuhn and Moshman argue in their respective contributions to this special issue, we need both constructs in order to understand the complex nature of what truly develops in reasoning. This is particularly relevant when early competence is examined. Most theories that make this claim look at fairly simple forms of reasoning. One important example is Braine's natural logic theory (Braine, 1978), which claims that there are some forms of reasoning that are essentially innate. These are quite straightforward forms of reasoning, such as the principle of modus ponens, which states that "If P then Q, P is true, then Q must be true". In fact, very young children consistently make this inference on a variety of premises. However, when more complex contexts are used, there is a clear developmental trend to fail to make the same inference (Simoneau & Markovits, 2003). There is no reason to believe that older adolescents and adults lose the ability to make the simple modus ponens inference. How then to explain the difference? Both Moshman and Kuhn et al. convincingly argue that the addition of more complex forms of information requires more complex forms of understanding and control. They claim that developmental complexity in reasoning is not additive, since it is not simply an accumulation of simple reasoning principles, but that coordinating and understanding complex forms of reasoning implies the development of meta-concepts and corresponding forms of executive control. When young children's performance on complex tasks requiring argumentation and understanding of basic logical metaconcepts is compared to that of adults, the developmental difference between them becomes very clear. As Kuhn et al. also argue, the same difference can be found when comparing "good" and "bad" reasoners of the same age. These two papers convincing argue that one of the key problems with most contemporary accounts of reasoning is a failure to provide for explicit higher-level procedures and concepts, a failure that is compounded by selective blindness as to the nature of developmental change.

This special issue thus offers a varied and almost exhaustive overview of the different ways to fill the theoretical and empirical gaps between studies of children's reasoning and studies of adult reasoning and to solve the apparent contradiction between young children's competence and adults' "incompetence". We hope that it will constitute a step towards a renewal of the tradition of the developmental study of reasoning, which remains an important and privileged means for understanding human cognition.

REFERENCES

Baillargeon, R., & DeVos, J. (1991). Object permanence in young infants: Further evidence. *Child Development, 62*(6), 1227–1246.

Barrouillet, P., & Lecas, J. F. (1999). Mental models in conditional reasoning and working memory. *Thinking and Reasoning, 5*(4), 289–302.

Braine, M. D. S. (1978). On the relation between the natural logic of reasoning and standard logic. *Psychological Review, 85*, 1–21.

Braine, M. D. S., & O'Brien, D. P. (1991). A theory of *if*: Lexical entry, reasoning program, and pragmatic principles. *Psychological Review, 98*, 182–203.

Bryant, P. E., & Trabasso, T. (1971). Transitive inferences and memory in young children. *Nature, 232*, 456–458.

Case, R. (1985). *Intellectual development: Birth to adulthood.* New York: Academic Press.

Case, R. (1992). *The mind's staircase: Exploring the conceptual underpinnings of children's thought and knowledge.* Hillsdale, NJ: Lawrence Erlbaum Associates Inc.

Dias, M. G., & Harris, P. L. (1988). The effect of make-believe play on deductive reasoning. *British Journal of Developmental Psychology, 6*, 207–221.

Evans, J. St. B. T. (1989). *Bias in human reasoning: Causes and consequences.* Hove, UK: Lawrence Erlbaum Associates Ltd.

Evans, J. B. St. T., & Over, D. E. (1996). *Reasoning and rationality.* Hove, UK: Psychology Press.

George, C. (1997). Reasoning from uncertain premises. *Thinking & Reasoning, 3*, 161–189.

Halford, G. S., Wilson, W. H., & Phillips, S. (1998). Processing capacity defined by relational complexity: Implications for comparative, developmental, and cognitive psychology. *Behavioral and Brain Sciences, 21*, 803–864.

Harris, P. L., & Nunez, M. (1996). Understanding of permission rules by preschool children. *Child Development, 67,* 1572–1591.

Hawkins, J., Pea, R. D., Glick, J., & Scribner, S. (1984). "Merds that laugh don't like mushrooms": Evidence for deductive reasoning by preschoolers. *Developmental Psychology, 20*(4), 584–594.

Inhelder, B., & Piaget, J. (1958). *The growth of logical thinking from childhood to adolescence.* New York: Basic Books.

Johnson-Laird, P. N., & Byrne, R. M. J. (2002). Conditionals: A theory of meaning, pragmatics, and inference, *Psychological Review, 109*(4), 646–678.

Kuhn, D. (1977). Conditional reasoning in children. *Developmental Psychology, 13,* 342–353.

Leevers, H., & Harris, P. (1999). Transient and persisting effects of instruction on young children's syllogistic reasoning with incongruent and abstract premises. *Thinking and Reasoning, 5*(2), 145–174.

Markovits, H., & Barrouillet, P. (2002). The development of conditional reasoning: A mental model account. *Developmental Review, 22,* 5–36.

Markovits, H., & Doyon, C. (in press). Information processing and reasoning with premises that are not empirically true: Interference, working memory and processing speed. *Memory and Cognition.*

Markovits, H., Venet, M., Janveau-Brennan, G., Malfait, N., Pion, N., & Vadeboncoeur, I. (1996). Reasoning in young children: Fantasy and information retrieval. *Child Development, 67,* 2857–2872.

Pascual-Leone, J. A. (1970). A mathematical model for the transition rule in Piaget's developmental stage. *Acta Psychologica, 32,* 301–345.

Pears, R., & Bryant, P. (1990). Transitive inferences by young children about spatial position. *British Journal of Psychology, 81,* 497–510.

Reber, A. S. (1993). *Implicit learning and tacit knowledge.* New York: Oxford University Press.

Rumain, B., Connell, J., & Braine, M. D. S. (1983). Conversational comprehension processes are responsible for reasoning fallacies in children as well as adults. *Developmental Psychology, 19,* 471–481.

Saffran, J. R., Aslin, R. N., & Newport, E. L. (1996). Statistical learning by 8-month-old infants. *Science, 274,* 1926–1928.

Simoneau, M., & Markovits, H. (2003). Reasoning with premises that are not empirically true: Evidence for the role of inhibition and retrieval. *Developmental Psychology, 39*(6), 964–975.

Sloman, S. A. (1996). The empirical case for two systems of reasoning. *Psychological Review, 1,* 3–22.

Stanovich, K. E., & West, R. F. (1997). Reasoning independently of prior belief and individual differences in actively open-minded thinking. *Journal of Educational Psychology, 89,* 342–357.

Stanovich, K. E., & West, R. F. (1998). Individual differences in rational thought. *Journal of Experimental Psychology: General, 127,* 161–188.

Stanovich, K. E., & West, R. F. (2000). Individual differences in reasoning: Implications for the rationality debate? *Behavioral and Brain Sciences, 23,* 645–665.

Vinter, A., & Detable, C. (2003). Implicit learning in children and adolescents with mental retardation. *American Journal of Mental Retardation, 108,* 94–107.

Vinter, A., & Perruchet, P. (2000). Implicit learning in children is not related to age: Evidence from drawing behavior. *Child Development, 71,* 1223–1240.

Von Fersen, L., Wynne, C. D. L., Delius, J. D., & Staddon, J. E. R. (1991). Transitive inference formation in pigeons. *Journal of Experimental Psychology: Animal Behavior Processes, 17*(3), 334–341.

Wason, P. C. (1968). Reasoning about a rule. *Quarterly Journal of Experimental Psychology, 20,* 273–281.

THINKING & REASONING, 2004, *10* (2), 123–145

The development of deductive reasoning: How important is complexity?

Graeme S. Halford
University of Queensland, Australia

Glenda Andrews
Griffith University, Brisbane, Australia

Current conceptions of the nature of human reasoning make it no longer tenable to assess children's inference by reference to the norms of logical inference. Alternatively, the complexity of the mental models employed in children's inferences can be analysed. This approach is applied to transitive inference, class inclusion, categorical induction, theory of mind, oddity, categorical syllogisms, analogy, and reasoning deficits. It is argued that a coherent account of children's reasoning emerges in that there is correspondence between tasks at the same level of complexity across different domains, and that the inferences of younger children, while impressive and important, are consistently simpler than those of older children.

Our conceptions of the nature of children's reasoning have undergone a number of highly significant changes in the last few decades. Piaget's very elaborate and influential conception was essentially based on psycho-logic. Piaget (1950) suggested that "logic is the mirror of thought" (p. 27), meaning that logic reflects properties that are inherent in thought. However research in the latter half of the twentieth century resulted in a number of alternative conceptions of human thinking. Some of the most notable of these were the information processing model (Anderson, 1983; Newell & Simon, 1972), reasoning based on heuristics (Kahneman, Slovic, & Tversky, 1982), a conception based on "mental models" (Johnson-Laird & Byrne, 1991), and the rational analysis approach (Anderson, 1990, 1991).

Information processing theories did not entail strong assumptions about humans as logical reasoners, but were based on complex problem-solving algorithms that were tested by computer simulation. Production system

Correspondence should be addressed to Graeme Halford, School of Psychology, University of Queensland, 4072, Australia. Email: gsh@psy.uq.edu.au

http://www.tandf.co.uk/journals/pp/13546783.html   DOI: 10.1080/13546780442000033

models (Anderson, 1983; Newell & Simon, 1972) were even less constrained by theories of logical reasoning, the only strong assumption being that human reasoners used condition-action rules. Neural net models (Rumelhart & McClelland, 1986) moved even further from conceptions based on psycho-logic, to one based on parallel acting constraints.

The mental models approach originated from many sources but one of the most complete mental models theories was that of Johnson-Laird and his collaborators on categorical syllogisms (Johnson-Laird, 1983; Johnson-Laird & Byrne, 1991). A mental model is a representation that is usually content-specific, and which is an analogue of the structure in the problem. Thus the adoption of a mental models approach represented a shift away from conceptions based on logical rules of universal validity towards representations that were specific to particular content domains. An intermediate position was developed by Cheng and Holyoak (1985) based on pragmatic reasoning schemas. These include schemas such as permission and obligation, which have wide applicability and are induced from life experience. Both the mental models and pragmatic reasoning schema approaches were enhanced by the development of analogy theory. Analogy appears to be fundamental to human reasoning (Hofstadter, 2001) which might be considered more analogical than logical (Halford, 1993).

The discovery of some important reasoning heuristics by Kahneman & Tversky (1973; Tversky & Kahneman, 1973) suggested that some human reasoning was even in contradiction of logical and statistical rules. This interpretation has been questioned by Cohen (1981). Another important implication of Kahneman and Tversky's approach is that it highlights the role of memory in human reasoning. For example we judge the likelihood of a class of entities or events by the ease with which they can be retrieved from memory. A fundamental change to the way human rationality is defined was brought about by the approach of Anderson, to be considered next.

The rational analysis approach (Anderson, 1990, 1991) regards reasoning as rational to the extent that it serves the needs of the organism in its adaptation to the environment. This fundamental shift in the definition of the rational response to a problem means that responses that are considered wrong or illogical by normative criteria might sometimes be considered rational if they are consistent with the person's interpretation of the situation, and if the information environment is taken into account. To some extent, this reconciles the arguments of Kahmenan and Tversky (1973) and Cohen (1981).

The development of these alternative conceptions of human reasoning meant that children's reasoning could no longer be assessed by the criteria of normative logic, although assessments of logical reasoning are still made (Rips, 2001; Smith, 2002). An alternative is to assess children's reasoning according to the complexity of the inferences they make. This approach has reached the point where it can bring some order to the field, enabling a number of paradoxes to be resolved. We will explore this development in this paper.

THE IMPACT OF MENTAL MODELS: THE CASE OF TRANSITIVE INFERENCE

Mental models accounts of the development of reasoning have now been proposed in a number of domains, including categorical syllogisms (Johnson-Laird, 1983; Johnson-Laird & Byrne, 1991), conditional reasoning (Markovits & Barrouillet, 2002), the Wason selection task (Cheng & Holyoak, 1985), and the concept of the earth (Vosniadou & Brewer, 1993). However, first we will consider models of transitive inference in some detail because it has been an important concept in cognitive development research, and is a good illustration of both mental models and cognitive complexity.

Transitive inference means that if R is a transitive relation, then aRb and $bRc \rightarrow aRc$ (e.g., $>$ is a transitive relation, so $a > b$ and $b > c$ implies $a > c$). Transitivity was regarded by Piaget (1971) as a case of logical reasoning but subsequent work showed that it was performed by creating a representation of the premise elements as an ordered set (Riley & Trabasso, 1974). They based their research on the paradigm of Bryant and Trabasso (1971), which consisted of teaching children the relative lengths of pairs of coloured sticks—that is $a < b$, $b < c$, $c < d$, $d < e$. They were then tested on all possible pairs. Even 4-year-olds were shown to recognise that $b < d$ better than chance, although they had not experienced this pair (and could not answer by the nontransitive strategy of labelling b as small and d as large, as can occur with end elements).

Riley and Trabasso (1974) extended the paradigm by adding a further pair, $e < f$, enabling a further inference $b < e$, to be tested. A logical reasoning model would imply that $b < e$ would be a harder than $b < d$ because $b < e$ requires the two-step inference: $b < c$, $c < d \rightarrow b < d$ and $b < d$, $d < e \rightarrow b < e$. Riley and Trabasso found the opposite: $b < e$ was *easier* than $b < d$. The reason was that participants performed the task by representing the elements as an ordered set, $a, b, c, d, e, (f)$. The elements b, e are more different in the representation, so the inference $b < e$ is easier because of the symbolic distance effect. Other evidence supported the conclusion that transitive inference was performed, not by logical reasoning, but by constructing a mental model comprising the ordered set of premise elements. The inference could be made simply by inspecting this mental model, a process that Thayer and Collyer (1978) described as "almost perceptual" (p. 1338).

This paradigm is potentially a valid test, because the transitivity principle is entailed in constructing the ordered set (an ordered set is one on which an asymmetric, transitive binary relation is defined). However the solution does not conform to a straightforward model of logical inference. Discoveries such as this were a watershed in cognitive development research because they showed that logical inference criteria are difficult to use as norms for children's reasoning. A different approach is required.

This example illustrates that a viable alternative to the logical inference conception of reasoning is to examine the cognitive processes used. In this case, the discovery that the task is performed by representing the premises as an ordered set, was a valuable insight, and one that generated a lot of research (Andrews & Halford, 1998; Breslow, 1981; Foos, Smith, Sabol, & Mynatt, 1976; Pears & Bryant, 1990). The process of constructing the ordered set representation is an important part of the reasoning process, because it is there that the transitivity principle has to be applied, at least implicitly. Because the ordered set mental model is constructed while learning the premises, training on the premises needed to be scrutinised in order to assess the validity of assessments. In the Bryant and Trabasso (1971) paradigm participants were given many trials on the adjacent pairs, which were presented initially in ascending order, $a < b$, $b < c$ etc., or the reverse. The trouble is that this helps children construct the ordered set, which is the real cognitive work of the task. Children who did not learn the pairs were eliminated, but this could reflect their inability to construct the representation, which is the true test of transitive inference. When these factors were eliminated, children under 5 years were not found to succeed (Halford & Kelly, 1984; Kallio, 1982).

Repeated presentation of the premises, often over hundreds of trials, also permits simplifying strategies. For example, a can be identified as an end element because it is always *less*, whereas e (f) can be identified as an end element because it is always *more*. Once an end element is identified, the rest of the ordered set can be constructed by concatenation. With a as an end element, and given $a < b$, we can form the string a, b, then with $b < c$ we can add c, yielding a, b, c, and so on. The question is: Given that this strategy is possible, is this paradigm a legitimate way to assess transitive inference? It is very hard to answer this question, because our only criterion for legitimacy is the transitivity principle, which can be implemented in many different ways, and it probably serves no useful purpose to call some of them legitimate and some not. The demonstrated validity of the mental models account of transitive inference means we can no longer determine the validity assessments by reference to norms of logical reasoning. However, we can ask whether it is a simpler process than that which is involved in some other transitive inference tasks. For this we need a complexity metric, to which we turn next.

COMPLEXITY OF COGNITIVE PROCESSES

There are currently two metrics for complexity in reasoning. One of these is cognitive complexity and control theory (Frye, Zelazo, & Burack, 1998; Zelazo & Frye, 1998; Zelazo, Frye, & Rapus, 1996) and the other is relational complexity theory (Halford, Wilson, & Phillips, 1998b).

Cognitive complexity and control (CCC) theory

CCC theory was developed to account for difficulties that preschool children were observed to have with a number of tasks, including the dimensional change card sort (DCCS) task. The DCCS requires children to sort coloured shapes into two piles according to explicitly stated rule sets. Participants are shown two template cards (e.g., a blue triangle and a green square) and are given sort cards that differ from template cards on one dimension (e.g., a blue square and a green triangle). If children are playing the "colour" game, they are instructed to place green sort cards beneath the green square template card and blue sort cards beneath the blue triangle template card, resulting in a match by colour. After several trials of the colour game, participants are told to play the "shape" game, and are instructed to place the blue square sort card beneath the green square template card and the green triangle sort card below the blue triangle template card. Research indicates that preschoolers sort successfully under the first set of rules (e.g., colour) but experience difficulty switching between dimensions (e.g., from colour to shape).

According to CCC theory, preschoolers can represent simple rules of the form "if Attribute A then Category C". Therefore they can perform classification tasks according to a rule such as "if red then sort with red triangle". That is, they can form the $A \rightarrow C$ links shown in Figure 1. However they do not consider the rules in relation to other rules and embed them under higher-order rules. The switch from one game to another requires that $A \rightarrow C$ links be embedded under setting conditions, S_1/S_2, which control the switch from the colour game to the shape game. Embedding the $A \rightarrow C$ links under the setting condition forms a higher-order rule, as shown in Figure 1 (Zelazo & Frye, 1998).

According to this theory, complexity corresponds to number of the levels of rule embedding required to solve the task successfully. The complex, higher-order rule corresponds to three levels of the hierarchy, whereas the simpler rules correspond to two levels. It is not until 4 to 5 years of age that children are able to represent higher-order rules (Frye, Zelazo, & Palfai, 1995).

A.

Template

C_1 — triangle "blue"

C_2 — square "green"

Colour game (S_1)

A_1 — square "blue"

A_2 — triangle "green"

Shape game (S_2)

A_2 — triangle "green"

A_1 — square "blue"

B.

S_1 S_2

A_1 A_2 A_1 A_2

C_1 C_2 C_2 C_1

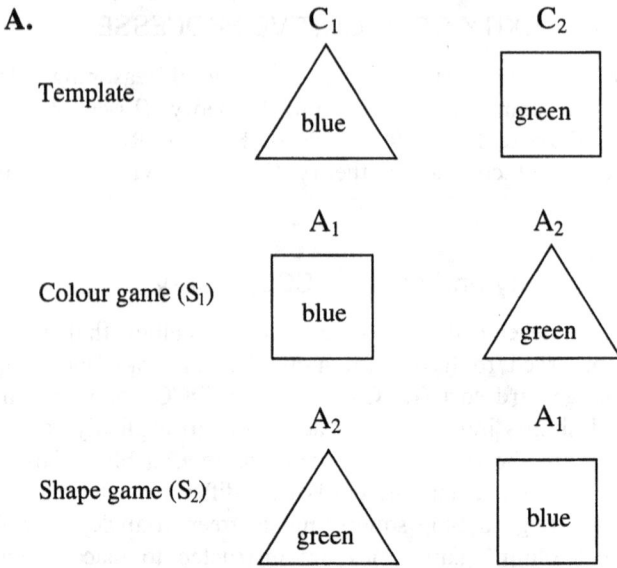

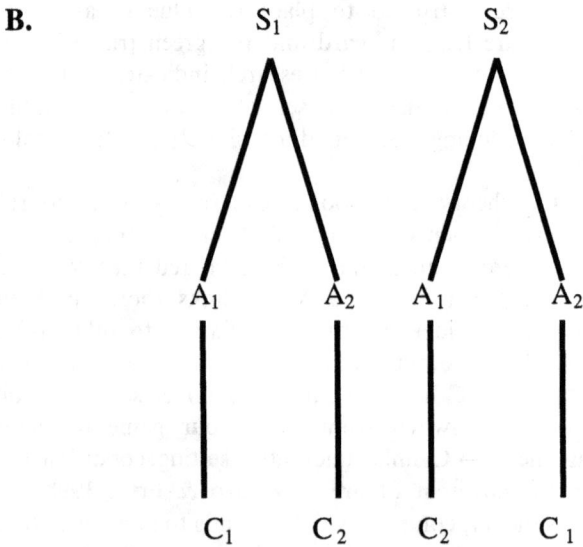

Interaction between S_1/S_2 and A_1/A_2 constrains decomposition.

Figure 1. Embedded rules analysis of Dimensional Change Card Sorting task, where S means setting condition, A means attribute, and C indicates the classification decision. Adapted from Frye, Zelazo, and Palfai (1995).

Relational complexity (RC) theory

RC theory (Halford et al., 1998b) defines complexity as a function, not of the total information in a task, but of the number of variables that can be related in a single cognitive representation. This corresponds to the *arity*, or number of arguments (slots) of a relation. The representation of a binary relation such as "larger than" has two slots, one for a larger and one for a smaller entity. Each slot can be filled in a number of ways: larger-than(elephant,mouse), larger-than(ship,canoe), larger-than(mountain,mole-hill). Therefore each slot corresponds to a variable or a dimension that can take a number of values. In general, an n-ary relation is a set of points in n-dimensional space.

Data in the literature, and from our laboratory, indicate that the median ages of attainment for unary, binary, ternary and quaternary relations are 1 year, 2 years, 5 years, and 11 years, respectively. Quaternary relations are the most complex that can be processed in parallel by most adult humans, although a minority can process quinary relations under optimal conditions.

CCC theory and RC theory developed in parallel and have some common ground. The principal difference is that whereas complexity in CCC theory is based on the number of levels of embedding of a set of rules, in RC theory it is based on the number of variables required to define a cognitive representation. Some translation between theories is possible, because extra levels of embedding correspond to additional variables. For example, we can express the hierarchy in Figure 1 by the set of ordered 3-tuples DCCS = {(S1, A1, C1), (S1, A2, C2), (S2, A1, C2), (S2, A2, C1)}. This relates three variables, S, A, C, and is a ternary relation. RC theory can handle both hierarchically structured and nonhierarchical cognitive tasks (Halford et al., 1998b).

Analysis of RC is based on a model of the cognitive processes employed in the task. Models must be verified independently and objectivity of complexity analyses is a direct function of the precision of process models. The principles for complexity analysis are codified in the Method for Analysis of Relational Complexity (MARC) and take account of expertise and cognitive strategies that influence information processing efficiency.

The prerequisites for RC analyses are that (a) the tasks used are appropriate for the age and/or species of participants; (b) training or familiarisation is employed to ensure participants are familiar with materials, procedure and task demands, and have the requisite declarative and procedural knowledge; and (c) control tasks are included to assess performance with materials and procedures (e.g., use closely matched binary relations tests when assessing ternary-relational processes).

It has been a major difficulty for cognitive complexity analyses that humans have very proficient strategies to reduce processing loads. MARC includes an objective basis for predicting when processing complexity can be reduced (Halford & Andrews, 2001). Complex tasks are *segmented* into components that do not overload capacity to process information in parallel. However relations between variables in different segments become inaccessible (just as a three-way interaction would be inaccessible if two-way analyses were performed). Processing loads can also be reduced by *conceptual chunking,* which is equivalent to compressing variables (analogous to collapsing factors in a multivariate experimental design). For example, velocity = distance/time, but can be recoded to a binding between a variable and a constant (e.g., speed = 80 kph) (Halford et al., 1998b, Section 3.4.1). Conceptual chunking reduces processing load, but chunked relations become inaccessible (e.g., if we think of velocity as a single variable, we cannot determine what happens to velocity if we travel the same distance in half the time).

Complexity analyses are based on the principle that *variables can be chunked or segmented only if relations between them do not need to be processed.* Tasks that impose high loads are those where chunking and segmentation are constrained. For example, RC theory accounts for the difficulty of the DCCS task because it cannot be segmented into two subtasks that are performed serially, since the conflicting dimension is always present. That is, the setting condition must be processed along with the card attribute when sorting (e.g., it is necessary to keep in mind that we are sorting by colour in order to determine that the green circle is sorted with the green triangle). When the DCCS was modified so that it can be segmented, though retaining its hierarchical structure, the difficulty disappeared, as predicted by RC theory (Halford & Bowman, 2003; Halford, Bowman, McCredden, Cummins, & Zielinski, 2004b). Conceptual chunking and segmentation, and the principles that govern decomposability of cognitive tasks, are important ways in which RC theory differs from CCC theory.

COMPLEXITY ANALYSIS OF TRANSITIVE INFERENCE

The logic of RC theory can be illustrated by transitive inference. For this we will use an assessment procedure developed by Andrews and Halford (1998) based on a task used by Pears and Bryant (1990). A sample problem is shown in Figure 2. Transitive reasoning requires that the relations *green above red* and *red above blue* be integrated to form an ordered triple, *green above red above blue. Red above blue* can be deduced from this. How do we apply RC theory in order to quantify the complexity of this process? Notice that premise integration entails assigning entities to three slots in the same decision. For example, the

Premises

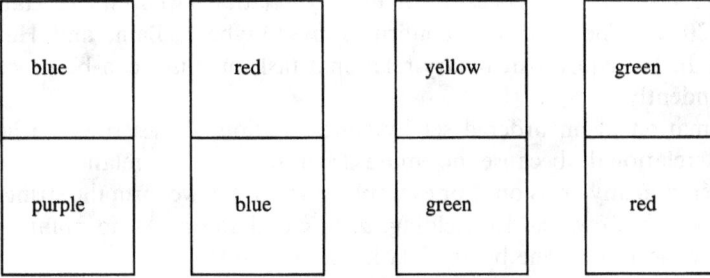

(A)

Binary items

Ternary items

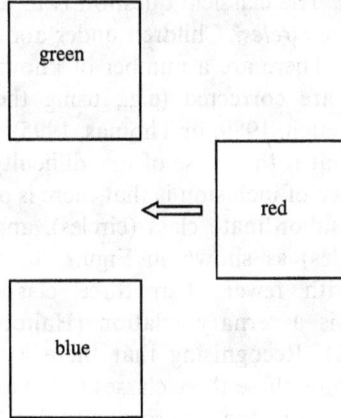

(B)

Figure 2. (A) An example premise display for the transitivity task. (B) The binary-relational items required construction of a five-square tower, placing adjacent squares in succession. The ternary-relational items required placement of nonadjacent squares (green, blue) followed by the intermediate square (red).

premise *green above red* implies green must be in the top or middle slot, but the second premise *red above blue* is required to determine that green must be in the top slot. Neither premise alone is sufficient to assign any element uniquely to one slot. Premise integration relates three variables, and the task entails processing a ternary relation (Andrews & Halford, 1998, 2002). The load was confirmed by Maybery, Bain, and Halford (1986). In the equivalent binary-relational task premises can be processed independently.

Formation of an ordered set by concatenation, as described earlier, is binary relational, because no more than one binary relation need be considered in any decision. For example, given $a < b$ we form the string a, b, then given $b < c$ we add c yielding, a, b, c and so on. At no point do we consider more than one binary relation at a time.

By contrast, the transitivity of choice paradigm (Chalmers & McGonigle, 1984) entails no scale that would provide a logical basis for integration (Markovits & Dumas, 1992) and the use of multiple trials enables the task to be performed by association (Wynne, 1995).

COMPLEXITY ANALYSIS OF CLASS INCLUSION

Another task that has been similarly difficult is class inclusion, exemplified in Figure 3a. The classical question is to ask children: *Are there more blue things or more circles?* Children under about 5 years typically say there are more circles. There are a number of known sources of false negatives, but when these are corrected (e.g., using the procedures of Hodkin, 1987, Halford & Leitch, 1989, or Thomas, 1995) the task is still difficult for young children. What is the cause of this difficulty?

The essence of inclusion is that there is a superordinate class (blue in our example) a subordinate class (circles), and a complementary subordinate class (triangles) as shown in Figure 3b. We cannot define an inclusion hierarchy with fewer than three classes. Thus class inclusion, like transitivity, is a ternary relation (Halford, 1993; Halford, Andrews, & Jensen, 2002). Recognising that there are more blue things than circles entails assigning these three classes to the appropriate slots in the hierarchy. Blue is assigned to the superordinate slot because it includes triangles and circles. Thus the assignment of classes to slots in the hierarchy depends on processing the relations between the three classes, and is ternary-relational. This imposes a processing load that has been verified by Halford and Leitch (1989).

Transitivity and class inclusion are superficially different, yet they are structurally similar, and both entail ternary relations, as Figure 4 shows. This is an example of how tasks can have equivalent RC despite different domains and different test procedures.

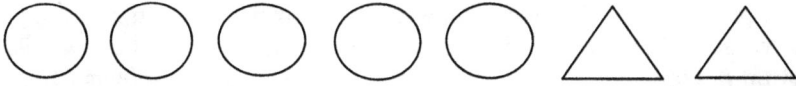

(A)

(B)

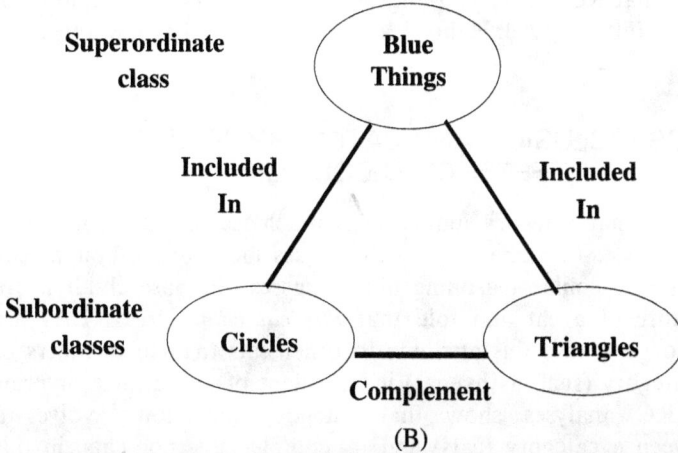

Figure 3. (A) An example display for the class inclusion task in which all objects are blue, and (B) the complexity of class inclusion.

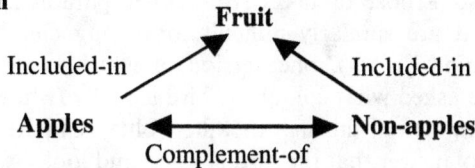

Figure 4. Transitivity and class inclusion are both ternary-relational.

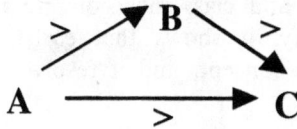

Transitivity and class inclusion were both originally Piagetian tasks, and the causes of children's failures have been controversial (Breslow, 1981; Bryant & Trabasso, 1971; Halford, 1993; Hodkin, 1987; Markovits, Dumas, & Malfait, 1995; McGarrigle, Grieve, & Hughes, 1978; Pears & Bryant, 1990; Siegel, McCabe, Brand, & Matthews, 1978; Thayer & Collyer, 1978), but after allowance is made for the numerous false negatives and false positives, there is a component of difficulty that still has to be explained. We have evidence that RC theory accounts well for this difficulty (Andrews & Halford, 1998; Halford, 1993; Halford & Leitch, 1989; Halford, Maybery, & Bain, 1986).

CLASS INCLUSION AND CATEGORY INDUCTION: A DIFFERENCE IN COMPLEXITY

It is a paradox that category induction is much less difficult for young children (Gelman & Markman, 1987) than class inclusion, although they appear to involve similar reasoning about classes. Suppose children are shown a picture of a cat and told that *this cat climbs trees*. They are more likely to generalise this attribute to other cats than to members of a different category (such as hyenas) independent of appearance or prior knowledge. RC analyses show that category induction involves a relation between a category (cats) and its complement (non-cats, in this case hyenas). This is a binary relation, whereas class inclusion is a ternary relation (Figure 5). A property inference procedure, carefully matched to that used with category induction, was developed to assess class inclusion. Consistent with RC theory, it was found that category induction was mastered by 3-year-olds whereas class inclusion was mastered at 5 years, and the latter was predicted by other ternary-relational tasks (Halford et al., 2002). The study demonstrates that category induction and class inclusion are really one paradigm at two levels of complexity, it shows that early competence is based on a structurally simpler concept, and it resolves a major discrepancy in the literature.

INFERENCES ABOUT MENTAL STATES

There is also a host of tasks from other paradigms that entail ternary relations and are similarly difficult for young children. One example is theory of mind (TOM), one version of which is illustrated in Figure 6. Children are asked what colour the bird is really (white), and what colour it appears when viewed through the filter (blue). Children below about 4 to 5 years tend to answer that the bird is white and looks white, or that it is blue and looks blue.

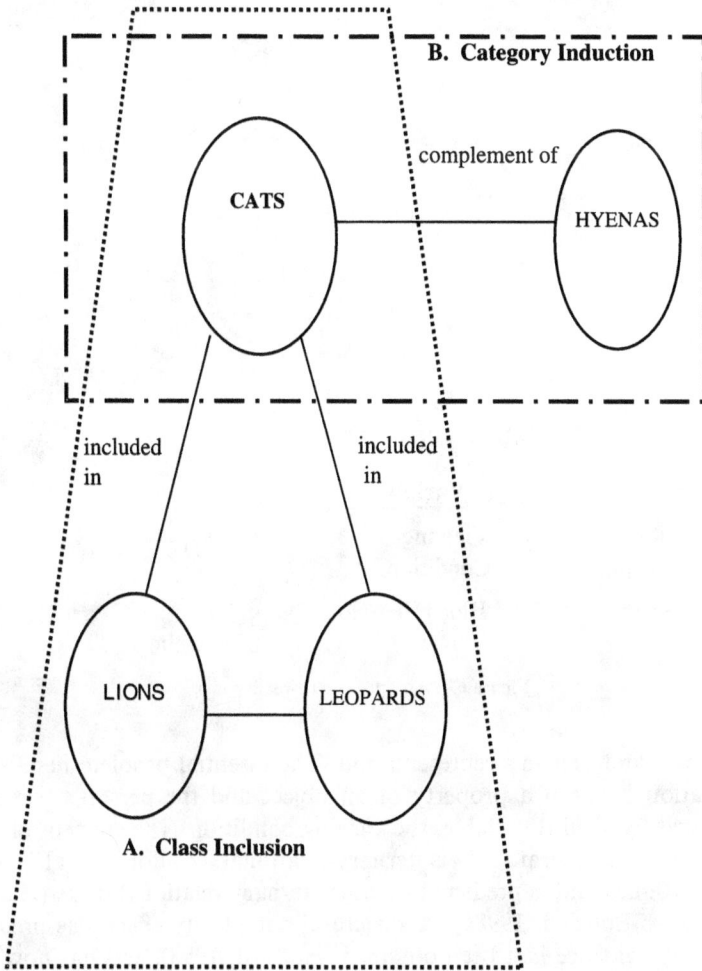

Figure 5.   Complexity of (A) class inclusion and (B) category induction

According to CCC theory, false belief and appearance-reality tasks are difficult for young children because they involve a pair of rules embedded under a higher-order rule. Empirical support for the approach comes from studies that have demonstrated significant associations between performance on TOM tasks and tasks such as the DCCS and ramp tasks (Carlson & Moses, 2001; Frye et al., 1995; Perner & Lang, 1999; Perner, Lang, & Kloo, 2002).

According to RC theory, false belief and appearance-reality tasks are difficult for young children because they relate three variables, environmental cue (e.g., an object attribute), setting condition (e.g., a viewing

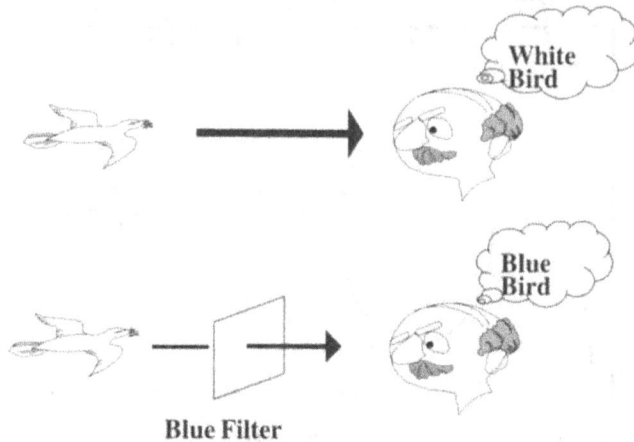

Variables

Object Attribute	Viewing Condition	Percept
"White"	Blue Filter/No Filter	See Blue/white

Figure 6. An appearance-reality task.

condition), and person's representation. The essential problem here is that the relation between a property of an object and the person's percept is modulated by a third variable, the viewing condition. The concept of mind task is complex because it is ternary-relational (Halford et al., 1998b, Section 6.2.4.3) and is predicted by other ternary-relational tasks (Halford, Andrews, & Bowden, 1998a). A structural complexity effect was predicted before any evidence had been obtained (Halford, 1993), and has now been confirmed (Davis & Pratt, 1995; Frye et al., 1995).

Andrews et al. (2003) reported three studies in which 3-, 4-, and 5-year-olds performed TOM tasks (false belief, appearance-reality) and predictor tasks from different content domains (transitivity, class inclusion, cardinality, hierarchical classification) with items at binary-relational and ternary-relational complexity levels. Performance on the RC predictor tasks accounted for more than 80% of age-related variance in TOM, and accounted for significant variance after age was partialled. Furthermore, the ternary-relational predictor task items accounted for TOM variance before and after controlling for binary-relational predictor items and binary-relational items from the TOM domain. The latter were of two kinds. Connections items were similar to Level 1 perspective-taking tasks previously used by Flavell, Green, and Flavell (1990). These items involve processing the link between the environmental cue and the person's representation. Based on such links children can specify whether objects in the environment are perceptible to themselves or to others, that is, whether a cognitive connection exists. Transformations tasks tested children's understanding the effects of location changes and coloured filters (e.g., that things appear blue when viewed through a blue filter). These items involved processing the link between the setting condition and the person's representation. Consistent with both CCC and RC theories, connections and transformations were easier and mastered earlier than TOM tasks.

CORRESPONDENCE ACROSS DOMAINS

It is an essential requirement for a complexity metric that tasks at the same level of complexity should be of equivalent difficulty across domains. This has been validated for binary- and ternary-relational tasks in the domains of transitivity, hierarchical classification, cardinality, comprehension of relative clause sentences, hypothesis testing and class inclusion (Andrews & Halford, 2002). Correspondence was observed between ages of attainment for tasks at the same RC level in these domains. All tasks loaded on a single factor that accounted for approximately 50% of the variance, and factor scores were correlated with age ($r = .80$), fluid intelligence ($r = .79$), and working memory ($r = .66$). Similar results were obtained recently for quaternary- and quinary-relational tasks in the domains of knights and knaves, latin square, N-back, Tower of Hanoi, and categorical syllogisms (Halford, Birney, Andrews, & Zielinski, 2004a) .

CATEGORICAL SYLLOGISMS

RC theory accounts for complexity in categorical syllogisms, although so far it has only been tested with adults in this domain. MARC is applied to categorical syllogisms by analysing the complexity of mental models used. Consider a syllogism: All A are B, all B are C. This is represented by Johnson-Laird and Byrne (1991, Table 6.1) as the mental model: $\{\{a\}b\}c$. This mental model can be expressed as ternary relation between the following classes: ABC, $\neg ABC$, $\neg A \neg BC$, where $\neg A$ means "not A" (Zielinski, Goodwin, & Halford, 2004). We can think of this as: The class ABC comprises entities A, that are B and C; the class $\neg ABC$ comprises entities B that are C but not-A; and the class $\neg A \neg BC$ comprises entities C that are not A and not B. Representation of the premises is equivalent to representing the relation between three classes of entities, and is ternary-relational. The categorical syllogism, Some A are B, No B are C express mutual constraints between five sets of elements: $A \neg BC$, $A \neg B \neg C$, $AB \neg C$, $\neg A \neg BC$, and $\neg AB \neg C$. This problem is therefore quinary-relational. The ternary relation problem is easier (88% correct) than the quinary problem (38% correct) according to data by Johnson-Laird and Byrne (1991). Johnson-Laird and Byrne explain this by number of mental models required (1 vs 3) but there is a lack of evidence that more than one model is constructed (Newstead, Handley, & Buck, 1999). MARC subsumes the mental models explanation, as Zielinski et al. (2004) have shown. To illustrate, of 27 syllogisms with valid conclusions, 7 are ternary-relational and require 1 mental model, and 17 that are more complex than ternary-relational entail more than 1 mental model (contingency coefficient $C = .61$).

ODDITY

RC theory yields predictions about children's understanding of oddity, based on the mental models children use. Simple oddity discrimination requires the child to select the odd object in a set of three or more. For example, in a set comprising one red and three blue circles, the odd object is the red circle. According to RC theory this would require processing binary relations because the identical stimuli can be chunked, as no relation between them needs to be processed. There is no recognition that the chunked stimuli, the three blue circles, are the same, but only that all are different from the odd stimulus. According to RC norms, simple oddity should be within the scope of children from 2 years of age.

In the dimension-abstracted oddity task, the non-odd stimuli are identical with respect to the relevant dimension, but differ on at least one other dimension. For example, the non-odd stimuli in a colour-relevant problem with two irrelevant dimensions might be a large red square, a small red triangle, and a medium red triangle, while the odd object is a large blue circle. By a logical reasoning account, selection of the odd object (large blue circle) requires a single dimension (colour) to be abstracted. This in turn requires recognition that the odd object is different from all the others, which are all the same as each other. As Chalmers and Halford (2003) point out, the three red objects cannot be chunked according to RC principles because the relation between them, sameness, must be processed. They show that the required mental model is equivalent to a ternary relation, it should impose a higher processing load, and should result in a later age of attainment. This is consistent with findings that dimension-abstracted oddity is more complex than simple oddity (Brown, 1970; Lubker & Small, 1969) especially for children under 5 years.

This analysis is based on an *a priori* logical reasoning account of the oddity concept. Investigation by Chalmers and Halford (2003) showed that there are strategies based on a simpler representation that produce an approximation to dimension-abstracted oddity. Such strategies must, of course, be verified independently, and their RC determined objectively, before they can be adopted as explanations. Children under 5 years were found to use a "simple oddity" strategy, in which an object that was different on any dimension was selected. Older children tended to use a "most different" strategy, based on the fact that the odd stimulus often differs most from the other stimuli in the set. In the dimension-abstracted oddity problem mentioned earlier, the odd object, the large blue circle, differs in a number of features from the large red square, the small red triangle, and the medium red triangle. Thus oddity can be detected by making a holistic comparison of features of the stimulus objects. Such a strategy is binary-relational because the only relation is between the odd object and the non-odd objects. The relation between the non-odd objects does not need to be processed, so they can be chunked according to RC analysis principles. As RC is not affected by the amount of information in each dimension, it is not influenced by number of features in the chunk. Comparison of the odd object with all the non-odd objects would be a holistic judgement (Smith, 1989) that would not entail explicit relational or dimensional information.

Older children's errors tended to be the stimulus that was the next most different from the other non-odd stimuli, and the problems with the highest error rates tended to be those that had the smallest difference between the most different (odd) and next most different stimulus. The children who showed these effects were those who were least able to detect "trick" problems in which there was no odd stimulus. Chalmers and Halford (2003) also found that young children were able to master generalised oddity discrimination, based on these simplified strategies.

This investigation of oddity understanding in children illustrates once again that analysis based on *a priori* logical principles can be misleading. A better approach is to empirically determine the mental models that are used, and to analyse their cognitive complexity.

ANALOGY

As analogy is basic to cognitive development, one of the important questions has been at what age it can be performed (Goswami, 1992; Halford, 1993; Halford et al., 1998b). The prediction that follows from RC theory is that analogy is possible when the relevant relations can be represented. Analogy is a mapping from a base or source to a target (Gentner, 1983), where both source and target are defined as sets of relations. A simple proportional analogy of the form $A:B::C:D$ (e.g., horse:foal::cat:kitten) is a mapping between two binary relations. Representation of both source and target does not increase processing complexity according to the principles of MARC because relational representations can be superimposed without increasing complexity, provided the relation between the source and target does not have to be explicitly represented. Consequently, analogies based on unary relations should be possible at 1 year, those based on binary relations should be possible from 2 years, and those based on ternary relations at 5 years. It is common ground that the requisite knowledge must be available.

Current data appear to be broadly consistent with this prediction. The most contentious prediction is that analogies based on ternary relations will not be possible before 5 years. For example, Goswami (1995) claims to have shown that 3- and 4-year-olds performed ternary-relational analogies, but Halford et al. (1998b) showed that Goswami failed to take account of simpler strategies that would account for the children's performance. Halford et al. (1998b) showed that one of the main findings claimed by Goswami (1995) was not statistically significant.

However one of the most important considerations is that complexity analysis must take account of the decomposability of tasks. An analogy based on a complex relation linking three variables will only be processed as ternary-relational if it is not possible to decompose the task into simpler subtasks. This has not been demonstrated in any of the research claiming to show ternary-relational analogical reasoning in young children, as far as we are aware.

REASONING DEFICITS

RC theory has not yet been extensively applied to patients with deficits in reasoning, although it has been an effective predictor of impairment in children with early-treated PKU (Jones, 2004). However it does appear to be effective in accounting for frontal lobe deficits (Christoff et al., 2001; Kroger, Sabb, Fales, Bookheimer, Cohen, & Holyoak, 2002; Waltz et al., 1999). Andrews and Halford (2002) explained how it could in principle account for typical deficits of patients with frontal lobe impairment as described by Luria (1973). The problem is: *There were 18 books on two shelves, but ... there were twice as many books on one shelf as the other.* Luria (1973, pp. 338–339) reports that frontal patients would either say there were 18 books on each shelf, or that there were 18 books on one shelf, and 36 books on the other. The task requires reasoning that there are 18 books on two shelves ($X + Y = 18$) and twice as many books on one shelf as the other ($2Y = X$). These notions each represent a binary operation, which is equivalent to a ternary relation. However the problem requires them to be integrated into a representation that expresses both relations, which is equivalent to $2y + y = 18$. This is an ordered 4-tuple $\{(2,y,y,18)\}$ and is equivalent to a quaternary relation. The attempted solutions are much simpler relations. The first amounts to two unary relations, that can be expressed as shelf-contents(18-books). They are two independent unary relations because the attempted solution does not utilise the relation between them. Therefore, by the principles of MARC, the representations can be segmented. The second attempt expresses 2y = x, a ternary relation, but this is not integrated with x + y = 18. By the principles of MARC, the solution process has the complexity of a ternary relation. Thus the inadequately planned problem solving by frontal patients can be interpreted as inability to process complex relations, a common result of which is to default to less complex relations.

ANIMAL COGNITION

RC theory has also been applied to cognition in higher animals, especially primates (Halford et al., 1998b). There is evidence that chimpanzees (*Pan Troglodytes*) can process binary relations, as indicated their performance on the generalised relational match-to-sample task (Thompson, Oden, & Boysen, 1997). However there is no evidence that they can process ternary relations. It would follow that chimpanzees could perform proportional analogies, and this has been confirmed empirically (Call & Tomasello, 1999). However they would not understand ternary-relational theory of mind tasks such as false belief. Although the literature on this issue has been controversial, some well-controlled studies (Call & Tomasello, 1999) tend to support this prediction.

WIDER IMPLICATIONS OF COMPLEXITY ANALYSIS

Given that developments in our understanding of human reasoning have made it no longer tenable to assess children's inferences solely by reference to the norms of logical inference, an alternative approach was needed. We have shown how complexity can be applied to the mental models used in a number of tasks that have been important in assessments of cognitive development. The invariable finding is that the inferences of younger children are less complex than those of older children. It is important that this does not deny that younger children make the inferences that have been reported, nor does it deny the importance of these performances. It does however help to resolve some paradoxes and bring some order to the field. Without a means of assigning cognitive tasks to equivalence classes, with common properties, and relating tasks in different classes to each other in an orderly way, psychology is in a similar position that of chemistry without the periodic table (Andrews & Halford, 2002; Frye & Zelazo, 1998) . While complexity analysis certainly does not resolve all the issues, it can perhaps be claimed to make a small step towards greater order in the field.

REFERENCES

Anderson, J. R. (1983). *The architecture of cognition.* Cambridge, MA: Harvard University Press.

Anderson, J. R. (1990). *The adaptive character of thought* (Vol. 1). Hillsdale, NJ: Lawrence Erlbaum Associates Inc.

Anderson, J. R. (1991). Is human cognition adaptive? *Behavioral and Brain Science, 14,* 471–517.

Andrews, G., & Halford, G. S. (1998). Children's ability to make transitive inferences: The importance of premise integration and structural complexity. *Cognitive Development, 13,* 479–513.

Andrews, G., & Halford, G. S. (2002). A cognitive complexity metric applied to cognitive development. *Cognitive Psychology, 45,* 153–219.

Andrews, G., Halford, G. S., Bunch, K. M., Bowden, D., & Jones, T. (2003). Theory of mind and relational complexity. *Child Development, 74,* 1476–1499.

Breslow, L. (1981). Reevaluation of the literature on the development of transitive inferences. *Psychological Bulletin, 89,* 325–351.

Brown, A. L. (1970). Transfer performance in children's oddity learning as a function of dimensional preference, shift paradigm, and overtraining. *Journal of Experimental Child Psychology, 9,* 307–319.

Bryant, P. E., & Trabasso, T. (1971). Transitive inferences and memory in young children. *Nature, 232,* 456–458.

Call, J., & Tomasello, M. (1999). A nonverbal false belief task: The performance of children and great apes. *Child Development, 70,* 381–395.

Carlson, S. M., & Moses, L. J. (2001). Individual differences in inhibitory control and children's theory of mind. *Child Development, 72,* 1032–1053.

Chalmers, K. A., & Halford, G. S. (2003). Young children's understanding of oddity: Reducing complexity by simple oddity and "most different" strategies. *Cognitive Development, 18,* 1–23.

Chalmers, M., & McGonigle, B. (1984). Are children any more logical than monkeys on the five-term series problem? *Journal of Experimental Child Psychology, 37,* 355–377.

Cheng, P. W., & Holyoak, K. J. (1985). Pragmatic reasoning schemas. *Cognitive Psychology, 17,* 391–416.

Christoff, K., Prabhakaran, V., Dorfman, J., Zhao, Z., Kroger, J., Holyoak, K. J. et al. (2001). Rostrolateral prefrontal cortex involvement in relational integration during reasoning. *Neuroimage, 14,* 1136–1149.

Cohen, L. J. (1981). Can human irrationality be experimentally demonstrated? *Behavioral and Brain Sciences, 4,* 317–370.

Davis, H. L., & Pratt, C. (1995). The development of children's theory of mind: The working memory explanation. *Australian Journal of Psychology, 47,* 25–31.

Flavell, J. H., Green, F. L., & Flavell, E. R. (1990). Developmental changes in young children's knowledge about the mind. *Cognitive Development, 5,* 1–27.

Foos, P. W., Smith, K. H., Sabol, M. A., & Mynatt, B. T. (1976). Constructive processes in simple linear order problems. *Journal of Experimental Psychology: Human Learning and Memory, 2,* 759–766.

Frye, D., & Zelazo, P. D. (1998). Complexity: From formal analysis to final action. *Behavioral and Brain Sciences, 21,* 836–837.

Frye, D., Zelazo, P. D., & Burack, J. A. (1998). Cognitive complexity and control: I. Theory of mind in typical and atypical development. *Current Directions in Psychological Science, 7,* 116–121.

Frye, D., Zelazo, P. D., & Palfai, T. (1995). Theory of mind and rule-based reasoning. *Cognitive Development, 10,* 483–527.

Gelman, S. A., & Markman, E. M. (1987). Young children's inductions from natural kinds: The role of categories and appearances. *Child Development, 58,* 1532–1541.

Gentner, D. (1983). Structure-mapping: A theoretical framework for analogy. *Cognitive Science, 7,* 155–170.

Goswami, U. (1992). *Analogical reasoning in children.* Hove, UK: Laurence Erlbaum Associates Ltd.

Goswami, U. (1995). Transitive relational mappings in three- and four-year-olds: The analogy of Goldilocks and the three bears. *Child Development, 66,* 877–892.

Halford, G. S. (1993). *Children's understanding: The development of mental models.* Hillsdale, NJ: Lawrence Erlbaum Associates Inc.

Halford, G. S., & Andrews, G. (2001, October 26–27). *Interaction between variables is the missing factor in cognitive complexity.* Paper presented at the Second biennial conference of the Cognitive Development Society, Virginia Beach, USA.

Halford, G. S., Andrews, G., & Bowden, D. (1998a, July 1–4). *Complexity as a factor in children's theory of mind.* Paper presented at the poster session of the XVth Biennial Conference of the International Society for the Study of Behavioral Development, Berne, Switzerland: ERIC document Accession number ED 421 673.

Halford, G. S., Andrews, G., & Jensen, I. (2002). Integration of category induction and hierarchical classification: One paradigm at two levels of complexity. *Journal of Cognition and Development, 3,* 143–177.

Halford, G. S., Birney, D. P., Andrews, G., & Zielinski, T. A. (2004a). *A computerised test of relational complexity.* Manuscript in preparation.

Halford, G. S., & Bowman, S. (2003). *Cognitive task difficulty: Hierarchical structure or indecomposability.* Paper presented at the 13th Biennial Conference of the Australasian Human Development Association, Auckland, New Zealand.

Halford, G. S., Bowman, S., McCredden, J. E., Cummins, T. D. R., & Zielinski, T. A. (2004b). *Cognitive task difficulty: Hierarchical structure or decomposition into subtasks.* Manuscript in preparation.

Halford, G. S., & Kelly, M. E. (1984). On the basis of early transitivity judgements. *Journal of Experimental Child Psychology, 38,* 42–63.

Halford, G. S., & Leitch, E. (1989). Processing load constraints: A structure-mapping approach. In M. A. Luszcz & T. Nettelbeck (Eds.), *Psychological development: Perspectives across the life-span* (pp. 151–159). Amsterdam: North-Holland.

Halford, G. S., Maybery, M. T., & Bain, J. D. (1986). Capacity limitations in children's reasoning: A dual task approach. *Child Development, 57,* 616–627.

Halford, G. S., Wilson, W. H., & Phillips, S. (1998b). Processing capacity defined by relational complexity: Implications for comparative, developmental, and cognitive psychology. *Behavioral and Brain Sciences, 21,* 803–831.

Hodkin, B. (1987). Performance model analysis in class inclusion: An illustration with two language conditions. *Developmental Psychology, 23,* 683–689.

Hofstadter, D. R. (2001). Analogy as the core of cognition. In D. Gentner, K. J. Holyoak, & B. N. Kokinov (Eds.), *The analogical mind: Perspectives from cognitive science* (pp. 499–538). Cambridge, MA: MIT Press.

Johnson-Laird, P. N. (1983). *Mental models.* Cambridge: Cambridge University Press.

Johnson-Laird, P. N., & Byrne, R. M. J. (1991). *Deduction.* Hove, UK: Lawrence Erlbaum Associates Inc.

Jones, T. (2004). *The contribution of cognitive capacity to executive functions in young children.* Manuscript in preparation.

Kahneman, D., Slovic, P., & Tversky, A. E. (1982). *Judgment under uncertainity: Heuristics and biases.* London: Cambridge University Press.

Kahneman, D., & Tversky, A. (1973). On the psychology of prediction. *Psychological Review, 80,* 237–251.

Kallio, K. D. (1982). Developmental change on a five-term transitive inference. *Journal of Experimental Child Psychology, 33,* 142–164.

Kroger, J., Sabb, F. W., Fales, C., Bookheimer, S. Y., Cohen, M. S., & Holyoak, K. (2002). Recruitment of anterior dorsolateral prefrontal cortex in human reasoning: A parametric study of relational complexity. *Cerebral Cortex, 12,* 477–485.

Lubker, B. J., & Small, M. Y. (1969). Children's performance on dimension abstracted oddity problems. *Developmental Psychology, 1,* 35–39.

Luria, A. R. (1973). *The working brain: An introduction to neuropsychology* (B. Haigh, Trans.). London: Penguin.

Markovits, H., & Barrouillet, P. (2002). The development of conditional reasoning: A mental model account. *Developmental Review, 22,* 5–36.

Markovits, H., & Dumas, C. (1992). Can pigeons really make transitive inferences? *Journal of Experimental Psychology: Animal Behavior Processes, 18,* 311–312.

Markovits, H., Dumas, C., & Malfait, N. (1995). Understanding transitivity of a spatial relationship: A developmental analysis. *Journal of Experimental Child Psychology, 59,* 124–141.

Maybery, M. T., Bain, J. D., & Halford, G. S. (1986). Information processing demands of transitive inference. *Journal of Experimental Psychology: Learning, Memory and Cognition, 12,* 600–613.

McGarrigle, J., Grieve, R., & Hughes, M. (1978). Interpreting inclusion: A contribution to the study of the child's cognitive and linguistic development. *Journal of Experimental Child Psychology, 26,* 528–550.

Newell, A., & Simon, H. A. (1972). *Human problem solving.* New York: Prentice-Hall.

Newstead, S. E., Handley, S. J., & Buck, E. (1999). Falsifying mental models: Testing the predictions of theories of syllogistic reasoning. *Memory & Cognition, 27,* 344–354.

Pears, R., & Bryant, P. (1990). Transitive inferences by young children about spatial position. *British Journal of Psychology, 81,* 497–510.

Perner, J., & Lang, B. (1999). Development of theory of mind and executive control. *Trends in Cognitive Sciences, 3,* 337–344.

Perner, J., Lang, B., & Kloo, D. (2002). Theory of mind and self-control: More than a common problem of inhibition. *Child Development, 73,* 752–767.

Piaget, J. (1950). *The psychology of intelligence.* (M. Piercy & D. E. Berlyne, Trans.) London: Routledge & Kegan Paul. [Original work published 1947.]

Piaget, J. (1971). *The theory of stages in cognitive development.* New York: McGraw Hill.

Riley, C. A., & Trabasso, T. (1974). Comparatives, logical structures and encoding in a transitive inference task. *Journal of Experimental Child Psychology, 17,* 187–203.

Rips, L. J. (2001). Two kinds of reasoning. *Psychological Science, 12,* 129–134.

Rumelhart, D. E., & McClelland, J. L. (Eds.). (1986). *Parallel distibruted processing: Explorations in the microstructure of cognition* (Vol. 1). Boston, MA: MIT Press.

Siegel, L. S., McCabe, A. E., Brand, J., & Matthews, J. (1978). Evidence for the understanding of class inclusion in preschool children: Linguistic factors and training effects. *Child Development, 49,* 688–693.

Smith, L. (1989). From global similarities to kinds of similarities: The construction of dimensions in development. In S. Vosniadou & A. Ortony (Eds.), *Similarity and analogical reasoning* (pp. 146–178). Cambridge: Cambridge University Press.

Smith, L. (2002). Piaget's model. In U. Goswami (Ed.), *Blackwell handbook of childhood cognitive development* (pp. 515–537). Cambridge, MA: Blackwell Publishing.

Thayer, E. S., & Collyer, C. E. (1978). The development of transitive inference: A review of recent approaches. *Psychological Bulletin, 85,* 1327–1343.

Thomas, H. (1995). Modeling class inclusion strategies. *Developmental Psychology, 31,* 170–179.

Thompson, R. K. R., Oden, D. L., & Boysen, S. T. (1997). Language-naive chimpanzees (*Pan troglodytes*) judge relations between relations in a conceptual matching-to-sample task. *Journal of Experimental Psychology: Animal Behavior Processes, 23,* 31–43.

Tversky, A., & Kahneman, D. (1973). Availability: A heuristic for judging frequency and probability. *Cognitive Psychology, 5,* 207–232.

Vosniadou, S., & Brewer, W. F. (1993). *Constraints on knowledge acquisition: Evidence from children's models of the earth and the day/night cycle.* Paper presented at the 15th Annual Conference of the Cognitive Science Society, University of Colorado, Boulder, CO, USA.

Waltz, J. A., Knowlton, B. J., Holyoak, K. J., Boone, K. B., Mishkin, F. S., de Menezes Santos, M. et al. (1999). A system for relational reasoning in human prefrontal cortex. *Psychological Science, 10,* 119–125.

Wynne, C. D. L. (1995). Reinforcement accounts for transitive inference performance. *Animal Learning and Behavior, 23,* 207–217.

Zelazo, P. D., & Frye, D. (1998). Cognitive complexity and control: II. The development of executive function in childhood. *Current Directions in Psychological Science, 7,* 121–126.

Zelazo, P. D., Frye, D., & Rapus, T. (1996). An age-related dissociation between knowing rules and using them. *Cognitive Development, 11,* 37–63.

Zielinski, T. A., Goodwin, G. P., & Halford, G. S. (2004). *Complexity of categorical syllogisms: A comparison of two metrics.* Manuscript submitted for publication.

THINKING & REASONING, 2004, *10* (2), 147–174

A dual-process approach to cognitive development: The case of children's understanding of sunk cost decisions

Paul A. Klaczynski and Jennifer M. Cottrell

The Pennsylvania State University

Only in recent years have developmental psychologists begun advocating and exploring dual-process theories and their applicability to cognitive development. In this paper, a dual-process model of developments in two processing systems—an "analytic" and an "experiential" system—is discussed. We emphasise the importance of "metacognitive intercession" and developments in this ability to override experiential processing. In each of two studies of sunk cost decisions, age-related developments in normative decisions were observed, as were declines in the use of a "waste not" heuristic. In the second study, children and adolescents were presented with arguments for normative and non-normative sunk cost decisions. Following argument evaluation, participants were re-presented the original problems and a set of novel, transfer problems. Results indicated that post-argument improvements were most apparent during adolescence. Age-related improvements were most noticeable on the transfer problems. In general, the findings suggest that the ability to metacognitively intercede (i.e., reflect on arguments; inhibit experientially produced responses) emerges towards middle adolescence. However, even by the end of adolescence, in the absence of significant contextual cues and motivation, this ability is infrequently utilised.

For decades, cognitive developmental psychology flourished under the guidance of Piaget's (1972; Inhelder & Piaget, 1958) general theory of intellectual development. Because Piaget's theory covered a wide range of intellectual domains—from simple sensorimotor skills to higher-order reasoning—and offered an equally impressive range of testable hypotheses, the theory opened innumerable avenues for empirical examination. Hundreds of empirical investigations dotted the developmental landscape, with many investigators claiming support for various Piagetian hypotheses

Correspondence should be addressed to Paul Klaczynski, Department of Psychology, The Pennsylvania State University, State College, PA, USA 16802. Email: pak21@psu.edu

http://www.tandf.co.uk/journals/pp/13546783.html   DOI: 10.1080/13546780442000042

and others claiming to have refuted aspects of Piaget's theory. As research proceeded from the 1970s and into the 1980s, and as the sheer quantity of anti-Piagetian evidence mounted, evidence taken as support of the theory was extensively criticised. Although many of these criticisms were unjustified and based on misinterpretations of basic Piagetian claims, by the mid-1980s it was clear that most cognitive developmentalists had serious misgivings about the adequacy of Piaget's approach.

As Piaget's theory fell from grace, information processing theories gained ground. However, although information processing theories remain in vogue, they have been criticised on several grounds. For instance, with few exceptions (e.g., Case, 1985, 1998; Markovits & Barrouillet, 2002), information processing theories have not provided adequate accounts of the mechanisms that guide developmental change. Obviously, this short-coming is critical for any adequate account of development. In addition, like other recent approaches to cognitive development (e.g., the "theory-theory" approach; see Wellman & Gelman, 1992), information processing theories either focused entirely on explicit information processing or ignored the implicit/explicit processing distinction.

In addition to these ongoing paradigm shifts, a disturbing trend in cognitive developmental research has been on determining the earliest ages at which particular abilities (e.g., "theory of mind") are in evidence. The general framework guiding much of this work has been, either implicitly or explicitly, nativist. Thus, rather than studying age-related change, some theorists (e.g., Gopnik & Wellman, 1994) have argued that very young children (e.g., 3- to 4-year-olds) possess abilities that are highly similar to the abilities of adults and that competencies once believed to emerge only during adolescence are, in fact, present in preschoolers (e.g., Ruffman, Perner, Olson, & Doherty, 1993).

As developmentalists' preoccupation with early development has continued, a number of interesting shifts have occurred in theories of adult cognition. In particular, adult theorists (e.g., Bargh & Chartland, 1999; Evans & Over, 1996; Stanovich, 1999) have recognised that reasoning and decision making are achieved largely through interactions between two processing systems. One system, here labelled the "analytic" system (see Evans, 1989), is concerned with conscious, explicit cognition. The second system, here referred to as the "experiential" system (see Epstein, 1994), operates at a minimally conscious level. With the exception of research on implicit and explicit memory (e.g., Lie & Newcombe, 1999; Schneider, & Bjorklund, 1998), cognitive developmentalists have assumed that a simple shift from predominantly intuitive processing to analytic processing is a principal characteristic of development and have focused their empirical efforts on developments in the analytic system. Thus, experiential processes have largely been ignored (Klaczynski, 2001a, in press-b).

In this paper, we first discuss the distinction between analytic and experiential processing. In doing so, we borrow heavily from the theories of Evans (1989; Evans & Over, 1996), Stanovich (1999; Stanovich & West, 2000), and Epstein (1994; Epstein & Pacini, 1999). This outline includes a discussion of the implications of dual-process theories for research on cognitive development. As an illustration of how dual-process theories can be applied to developmental phenomena, we then describe our research on the development of decisions based on sunk costs. Our conclusions focus on the role of analytic processing in overriding experiential processing and, specifically, on how developments in metacognitive abilities allow for age-related changes in the evaluation of preconsciously activated heuristics.

DUAL-PROCESS THEORIES OF REASONING AND DECISION MAKING

In contrast to traditional theories of development, a basic assumption of dual-process theories is that age-related change occurs in two separate operating systems. Rather than assuming that development proceeds from simple intuitive cognition to more computationally complex, deliberative cognition within a single operating system, dual-process theories assume that both deliberate, explicit processes and implicit, intuitive processes operate simultaneously at most, if not all ages (disentangling implicit from explicit cognition during infancy is likely to prove exceedingly difficult).

In the adult literature, dual-process theories arose because basic information processing theories and decision theories could not adequately account for the surprising finding that adults frequently perform poorly on a wide range of apparently simple judgement and reasoning tasks (e.g., conjunction problems, Wason's 1966 selection task). Although "bounded rationality" arguments provide one means of dealing with these findings—that is, by asserting that problem complexity often overwhelms human information processing capacities, thus forcing people to "do the best they can with what they have"—such arguments cannot explain developmental findings that children often perform well on the same tasks that seem to perplex adults (see Davidson, 1995; Jacobs & Potenza, 1991; Klaczynski & Narasimham, 1998; Markovits & Dumas, 1999; Reyna & Ellis, 1994). However, even if rationality (on simple problems) is bounded by information processing constraints, bounded rationality theories do not, in and of themselves, explain the precise means by which "satisficing" occurs.

Like competence/performance theories in developmental psychology (see Overton, 1985), dual-process theorists approach this problem by assuming that, even among individuals who possess the analytic competencies to solve complex tasks, these competencies are not always activated in situations that apparently call for their use. Instead, people typically rely on memory-based strategies that are activated by experiential system predominance. Task characteristics and individual differences in intellectual motivation (see Epstein & Pacini, 1999; Stanovich & West, 1997, 1998, 2000) determine which information processing system is predominant on that task. Because it is the more cognitively economical system, which emerged earlier in human evolution and often produces satisfactory (and sometimes optimal) responses, most theorists believe that the default processing system is experiential (Brainerd & Reyna, 2001; Evans & Over, 1996; Klaczynski, 2001b; Stanovich, 1999).

The experiential system involves the preconscious activation of procedural and episodic memories that can be used to guide judgements and decisions. Rather than relying on logical processing, when this system is predominant, people generally base their judgements on strongly activated memories. In general, experiential processing is fast, operates at a minimally conscious level, and places little, if any, demand on working memory. This system facilitates information mapping onto and assimilation into existing knowledge categories, operates to convert conscious strategies and tactics into automatic procedures, and aids the activation of decision-making heuristics and other memories (e.g., stereotypes, beliefs, vivid episodic memories) that bias judgements and interfere with attempts to reason "objectively".

Thus, experiential processing often depends on the activation of heuristic short-cuts, most of which are acquired through experience. Developmentally, this means that individuals' repertoire of heuristics should become increasingly diverse and more easily activated with age. The implication of this conclusion is *not* that adults will necessarily use heuristics more than children, but instead that—when experiential processing is predominant—adults' judgements and decisions will reflect more variability in the types of heuristics they use. If children have not yet acquired the heuristics that adults typically use on a task, the (possibly mistaken) conclusion that adults rely on experiential processing more than children may be drawn. However, simply because adults have more heuristics available than children does *not* mean that they will use heuristics more often. The high probability that an increasingly diverse array of heuristics is acquired from childhood through adulthood explains neither the frequency with which heuristics are applied to judgement and decision situations nor occasions on which heuristics, although activated, are not exercised. As discussed subsequently, because a situation activates a particular heuristic does not mean that this heuristic will be used. The experiential processing system, functioning with little or no conscious awareness, continuously assimilates information and matches internal and external cues to memory procedures; this matching process, in turn, activates and makes available specific heuristics for utilisation.

The experiential system co-develops with the analytic system. The analytic processing system comprises consciously controlled, effortful thinking, and the numerous competencies that have traditionally been considered essential to cognitive development and normative decision making (Evans & Over, 1996; Stanovich, 1999). Unlike experiential processing, analytic processing is directed towards breaking down problems into their component elements, examining these elements, and, from this analysis, deriving solutions, judgements, decisions, and arguments. In further contrast to experiential processing, analytic processing operates on "decontextualised" representations. The process of decontextualisation is essential if analytic competencies are to be engaged consistently and used effectively (Stanovich, 1999; Stanovich & West, 1997). Decontextualised task representations—wherein the underlying structure (e.g., logical components) of a problem is decoupled from superficial contents (e.g., counterfactual information)—provide a working memory structure on which logico-computational processing can operate (Stanovich & West, 1997; see also Donaldson, 1978). However, the ability to decontextualise task structure from potentially misleading contents, and from logically irrelevant memories activated by these contents, depends largely on the development of metacognitive and executive function abilities (e.g., impulse control, ability to inhibit memory-based interference). In Table 1 (adapted from Epstein, 1994; Evans, 2002; Stanovich, 1999), a brief list of the attributes of the two processing systems is presented.

As noted previously, development is in part characterised by the acquisition of judgement and decision heuristics. Although heuristics may

TABLE 1
Characteristics of the experiential and analytic processing systems

Experiential processing	Analytic processing
Evolved early	Evolved late
Fast	Deliberate
Automatic	Controlled and effortful
Minimally conscious	Conscious
Operates on contextualised representations	Operates on and constructs decontextualised representations
Involves activation of memories (e.g., beliefs, heuristics, stereotypes)	Involves activation of higher-order reasoning and decision-making abilities
Relies on cursory situational analyses	Relies on precision and breaking down situations into specific elements
Frees attentional resources for analytic processing	Heavy load on working memory
Operates independently from general intelligence	Operates in cooperation with general intelligence and metacognitive abilities

be learned explicitly, by and large they are acquired through implicit cognitive processes (see Reber, 1992). Once acquired, heuristics are activated automatically by situational cues. Many people also employ these heuristics automatically not only because they are "fast and frugal" (Gigerenzer, 1996), but also because they often lead to outcomes beneficial, or at least not harmful, to the decision-maker. Also, because people have only a fleeting awareness that they have been activated, and because their activation elicits intuitions or "gut" feelings that they are "right" for the immediate situation (Epstein, 1994), decision heuristics are often used in situations for which their relevance is doubtful. Yet, although heuristic activation is effortless and automatic, once activated, it is likely that some (but perhaps not all) heuristics are momentarily available in working memory (Klaczynski, 2001a, 2004, in press). This availability affords reasoners the opportunity to consciously reflect on the value of the heuristic and actively decide whether to use the heuristic or not. As the adult literature indicates, either most people do not engage in this type of conscious reflection or, if they do, most people decide that the heuristic is in fact worth using.

The first point of this discussion is that experiential processing tends to predominate people's thinking. Second, experiential processing predominance can be overridden by analytic processing (Stanovich, 1999). The process of overriding experiential processing is conscious, likely requires advanced metacognitive abilities, and therefore is likely to be achieved more effectively by adolescents and adults than by children. However, the third point of the foregoing discussion is that most adolescents (and most adults) are not predisposed to override the experiential system functioning; nonetheless, there are wide individual differences in the tendency to inhibit the utilisation of automatically activated heuristics, engage in logical analysis, and construct decontextualised task representations (Klaczynski, 2000; Stanovich & West, 2000).

We therefore argue that the acquisition of metacognitive abilities—and dispositional tendencies to *use* these abilities (see Stanovich, 1999)—is critical to managing the interface between analytic and experiential processing in working memory. Metacognitive competence comprises the abilities to reflect on the process of knowing, the structure and quality of evidence and strategies, and the accuracy of personal knowledge (Kuhn, 2000, 2001). Further, metacognitive abilities include the abilities to monitor reasoning for consistency and quality, inhibit memory-based interference in attempts to reason analytically, and evaluate the appropriateness of preconsciously activated heuristics (when these are available in working memory).

Developmental evidence thus points to two key distinctions between adult and child cognition. First, along with the obvious fact that adults possess more analytic competencies than children, adolescents and adults also have access to more heuristics. Because these heuristics have a longer history of use in adults than in children, it is very possible that heuristics become increasingly easy to activate with age (Klaczynski, 2004). Second, recent research indicates that perhaps the key difference between child and adolescent cognition concerns the greater likelihood that older individuals have acquired the various metacognitive abilities listed previously (see Moshman, 1990, 1999; Kuhn, 2000, 2001; Kuhn, Amsel, & O'Loughlin, 1988). However, as Kuhn's research illustrates, few adolescents and adults have fully acquired these abilities and, as the adult decision literature suggests, even fewer are disposed to using those metacognitive abilities they do possess.

APPLICATION TO DECISION MAKING: DEVELOPMENTAL TRENDS IN SUNK COST DECISIONS

Research on the development of decision making is still in its infancy. Although numerous investigations have examined adolescent decision making (e.g., Steinberg & Cauffman, 1996; see Jacobs & Ganzel, 1993), these investigations have typically focused more on specific issues (e.g., abortion) than on the actual processes that guide decision making (for exceptions, see Byrnes, 1998; Klaczynski, 2001a, 2001b; Kokis, Macpherson, Toplak, West, & Stanovich, 2002; Reyna & Ellis, 1994). The developmental literature on heuristics and biases is particularly sparse. Extant research has found that, at least under some conditions, and despite possessing the analytic competencies needed for normative solutions, adolescents and adults rely on certain heuristics (e.g., representativeness) more than children (see Davidson, 1995; Jacobs & Potenza, 1991; Klaczynski, 2000; Reyna & Ellis, 1994). However, as Kokis et al. (2002) and Klaczynski (in press) point out, these findings cannot be taken to mean that adolescents and adults *in general* rely more on experiential processing than children.

In two studies, we examined age-related changes in a particular heuristic—the "waste not" heuristic (see Arkes & Ayton, 1999; Baron, Granato, Spranca, & Teubal, 1993)—that adults frequently use when making decisions about "sunk costs". In Study 1, age trends in problems that did and did not involve sunk costs were explored. In Study 2, we employed the Stanovich and West (1999) methodology for studying the "understanding/acceptance" principle to examine age differences in the ability to reflect on arguments that were either against or in support of the "waste not" heuristic, the ability of different age groups to understand these arguments, and whether children applied their understanding of the arguments to subsequent sunk cost decisions.

Most theories of normative decision making maintain that anticipated future consequences, rather than investments in prior decisions, should be the primary determinants of current decisions (Arkes & Ayton, 1999). When sunk costs are "honoured" or the "sunk cost (SC) fallacy" is committed, decisions are dictated by inconsequential expenditures in prior actions (i.e., irretrievable time, money, effort, etc. "sunk" into a decision). Thus, after investing in a goal and subsequently discovering that the goal is no longer worthwhile, attainable, or as desirable as alternative goals, people continue "throwing good money [or effort] after bad" (Heath, 1995; Staw, 1976). For example, the more entrepreneurs invest in new businesses, the more likely they are to expand those businesses when they are failing (McCarthy, Schoorman, & Cooper, 1993).

Although considerable evidence indicates that adults commit the SC fallacy frequently, age differences in the propensity to honour sunk costs have been little studied. In their investigations of 7–15-year-olds (Study 1) and 5–12-year-olds (Study 2), Baron et al. (1993) found no relationship between age and SC decisions. By contrast, Klaczynski (2001b) reported that the SC fallacy decreased from early adolescence to adulthood, although normative decisions were infrequent across ages. A third pattern of findings is reviewed by Arkes and Ayton (1999). Specifically, Arkes and Ayton argue that two studies (Krouse, 1986; Webley & Plaiser, 1998) indicate that younger children commit the SC fallacy less frequently than older children.

Making sense of these conflicting findings is difficult because criticisms can be levied against each investigation. For instance, Arkes and Ayton (1999) questioned the null findings of Baron et al. (1993) because sample sizes were small (e.g., in Baron et al., Study 2, ns per age group ranged from 7 to 17). The problems used by Krouse (1986) and Webley and Plaiser (1998) were not, strictly speaking, SC problems (rather, they were problems of "mental accounting"; see Webley & Plaiser, 1998). Because Klaczynski (2001b) did not include children in his sample, the age trends he reported are limited to adolescence. Thus, an interpretable montage of age trends in SC decisions cannot be created from prior research.[1]

On the basis of the Krouse (1986) and Webley and Plaiser (1998) findings, and from other developmental findings indicating age-related increases in heuristic use, Arkes and Ayton (1999) hypothesised that children are likely less to commit the SC fallacy than adults. In part, the logic underlying this hypothesis is that, because they have had fewer experiences with precautions against waste (e.g., from parents, "eat all your food so it doesn't get

---

[1]The mean age of children in Study 1 of Baron et al. (1993) was 12.1 years. The standard reported deviation (1.6 yrs.) indicates that most children were between 10.5 and 13.7 years. Hence, small sample size could have interacted with a restricted age range to mask developmental differences.

wasted"), children have not fully internalised the "waste not" heuristic. As such, in contrast to adolescents and adults, the heuristic is less likely to be activated automatically and inappropriately applied in sunk cost situations. That is, although they may have knowledge of the heuristic, children may restrict their use of it to those specific situations in which it is, in fact, appropriate (e.g., buying more food than one can eat). Adults, by contrast, are more likely to apply the heuristic "thoughtlessly" in situations for which its usefulness is of doubtful value.

An alternative proposition is based on the previously outlined theory of the role of metacognition in mediating interactions between analytic and heuristic processing. In this view, even young children have had ample opportunities to convert the "waste not" heuristic from a conscious strategy to an automatically activated heuristic stored as a procedural memory. Evidence from children's experiences with food (e.g., Birch, Fisher, & Grimm-Thomas, 1999) provides some support for the argument that even preschoolers are frequently reinforced for not "wasting" food. Mothers commonly extort their children to "clean up their plates" even though they are sated and even though the nutritional effects of eating more than their bodies require are generally negative. If the "waste not" heuristic is automatically activated in sunk cost situations for both children and adults, then one possibility is that no age differences in committing the fallacy should be expected.

However, if activated heuristics are momentarily available for evaluation in working memory, then the superior metacognitive abilities of adolescents and adults should allow them to intercede in experiential processing before the heuristic is actually used. Although the evidence is clear that most adults do not take advantage of this opportunity for evaluation, the proportion of adolescents and adults who actively inhibit the "waste not" heuristic should be greater than the same proportion of children. The aim of Study 1 was to test these three competing hypotheses regarding the development of sunk cost decisions and, more generally, to illustrate the utility of adopting a dual-process approach to cognitive developmental phenomena.

STUDY 1

Method

Participants. As part of a larger study of decision making and its development, 30 7–8-year-old (13 boys, 17 girls; $M = 8.08$ yrs, $SD = 1.09$ yrs), 34 10–11-year-old (15 boys, 19 girls; $M = 10.84$ yrs, $SD = 0.63$ yrs), and 30 13–14-year-old (15 boys; 15 girls; $M = 13.80$ yrs, $SD = 0.93$ yrs) children participated. Participants were volunteers from private elementary and middle schools in central Pennsylvania. Experimental sessions were conducted with individual participants in rooms at their schools and lasted between 30 and 40 minutes.

Materials and procedure. Children made decisions on six sunk cost problems, which were intermixed with several other types of decision-making problems. Prior to each problem, participants were told that a story character needed help making a decision, that there was no right or wrong decision, and that it was important to recommend the decision that "you really think will be most helpful". To help the younger children understand the alternatives and to retain their attention, simple pictures accompanied the written descriptions of the alternatives. Presentation order of the decision options (i.e., the SC option and the "normative" non-SC option) within problems was counterbalanced across participants. The problems were presented in one of four randomly determined orders.

Of the six SC problems, two involved monetary investments, two involved time/effort investments, and two involved investments in projects with a peer. Each problem presented a decision that a hypothetical child had made, and the amount and type of investment that she or he had "sunk" into that decision. This decision was described as not likely to produce the effect for which it was intended. An alternative that was more likely to achieve the decision maker's goal was then presented.[2]

For each SC problem, a same-content, "no sunk cost" (N-SC) problem was created. N-SC problems described courses of action analogous to those in the SC problems, except that no decision to invest in these plans had been made. Pursuit of these plans would require the same amount and type of investment as in the analogous SC problems. An alternative plan that was more likely to achieve the decision maker's goal, and that had the same cost in the analogous SC problem, was also presented. The N-SC problems served as controls to ensure that, when children honoured sunk costs on the SC problems, they did so because of the investments that had been made and not because they misconstrued the decision maker's goals. Normative decisions (scored "1") in both the SC and N-SC problems were the options that were more likely to achieve the decision makers' goals.

Children made decisions on one SC problem and one N-SC problem from each domain (i.e., monetary, time/effort, peer). Thus, there were two

---

[2]From the normative perspective, the amount of time, effort, or money invested in a project should have no bearing on decisions to abandon or continue a decision. Psychologically, however, "amount" has a significant impact on the SC decisions of adults (McCarthy et al., 1993). Because the present research was largely exploratory, "amount" was not manipulated. Instead, the SC problems were piloted with adults to ensure that investments were sufficiently large to activate the sense that "a lot" would be "lost" if a decision were abandoned. Additional research is needed to determine whether, for example, children and adolescents have different thresholds for the level of investment required before they commit the SC fallacy.

problem sets, each containing three SC and three N-SC problems. The SC problems in one set were the N-SC problems in the other set and vice versa; approximately half of the children received one problem set and half received the other problem set. Problem set was a between-subjects variable; problem type (SC versus N-SC) and domain (monetary, time/effort, peer) were within-subjects variables. Because no effects of problem set were significant (smallest $p = .12$), this variable is not discussed further. Examples of SC and N-SC problems are presented in Appendix A.

Results

Mean scores are presented in Table 2. A 3 (age) × 3 (domain: monetary, effort, peer) × 2 (problem type: SC, N-SC) analysis of variance revealed an age-related increase in normative decisions across domains and problem types, $F(2, 104) = 6.02$, $p = .003$. In addition, the domain × problem type interaction was significant, $F(2, 208) = 8.73$, $p < .001$. Although SC scores did not differ on the monetary, time/effort, and peer problems ($p = .28$), N-SC scores were higher than SC scores on the monetary and time/effort problems ($ps < .001$), but not on the peer problems ($p = .06$). Thus, the SC fallacy was committed with significant frequency on the monetary and time/effort problems.

The results thus show age increases on both the SC and N-SC problems and, therefore, do not support the Arkes and Ayton (1999) hypothesis. However, despite significant age-related increases in normative decisions, scores on the SC problems were significantly below chance at each age (smallest $p = .038$). By contrast, N-SC scores were above chance for the 11- and 14-year-olds ($ps < .001$), but not the 8-year-olds (note, however, that

TABLE 2
Study 1: Age trends in sunk cost decisions in the monetary, effort, and friendship domains

Domain	8-year-olds	11-year-olds	14-year-olds
Money			
Costs sunk	.16 (.37)	.28 (.46)	.43 (.50)
No costs sunk	.61 (.50)	.74 (.44)	.84 (.37)
Time/Effort			
Costs sunk	.19 (.40)	.33 (.48)	.38 (.49)
No costs sunk	.52 (.51)	.77 (.43)	.81 (.40)
Friendship			
Sunk costs	.45 (.51)	.36 (.49)	.38 (.49)
No sunk costs	.42 (.50)	.51 (.51)	.57 (.50)

Scores could range from 0 to 1. Chance responding was .50.

the difference between N-SC scores and SC scores was significant, $ps < .001$, at all ages). Consistent with research on adults, most adolescents and children committed the SC fallacy in situations that involved investments in prior actions. This was particularly clear when those situations involved investments of effort and money. Figure 1 shows age trends in SC and N-SC decisions, collapsed across the monetary and time/effort domains. As the figure shows, age-related improvements in decision making occurred to very similar extents on the SC and N-SC problems. Also clear from the figure is that the SC fallacy was committed frequently across ages, but was especially common in the youngest age group (on approximately 82% of the problems, the 8-year-olds committed the fallacy).

Discussion

The findings support the notions that (a) analytic decision-making competencies improve from childhood to adolescence, at least in the domain of sunk cost decisions, but that (b) despite these improvements, most adolescents commit the sunk cost fallacy. Presumably, the fallacy is committed because—regardless of age—most children and adolescents apply an automatically activated heuristic against waste without evaluating

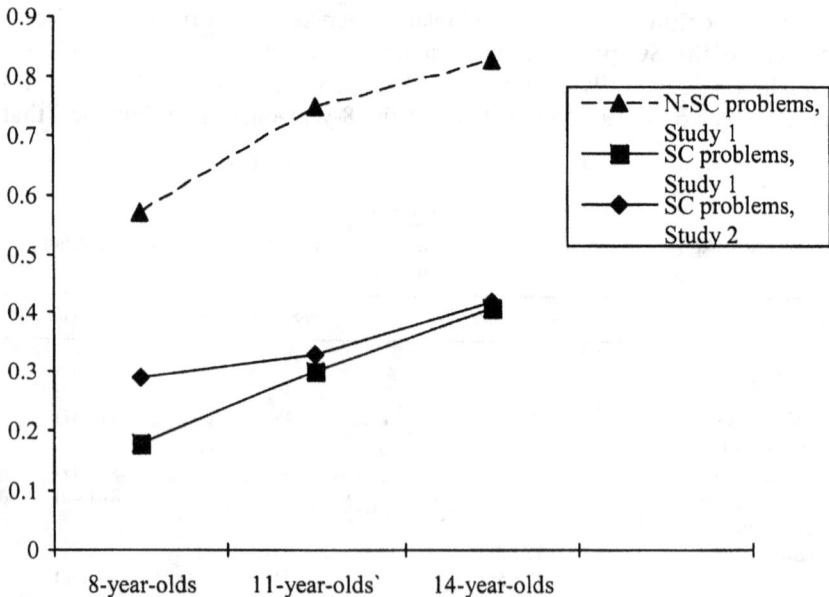

Figure 1. Age trends in SC and N-SC decisions across the monetary and effort domains.

its appropriateness to specific situations. The heuristic, in others words, operates as an all-purpose rule guarding against waste that is typically both activated and applied automatically. However, the developmental effect we observed could be at least partially attributed to improved abilities to inhibit experientially activated ("prepotent") heuristics. Thus, our suggestion is that the key difference between children and adolescents, at least on sunk cost decisions, is *not* their access to or the automaticity of the "waste not" heuristic"; rather, the difference is primarily in the ability to "metacognitively intercede" prior to applying the products of experiential processing (Klaczynski, 2004).

Alternatively, children may perform worse than adolescents because they simply do not understand the principle that decisions should be based on anticipated future consequences rather than prior investments. Because they do not possess the analytic competencies to make normative decisions, children rely on what they do know: the "waste not" heuristic. Opposed to this explanation, however, are the findings from the N-SC problems. On these problems, even the youngest participants performed significantly better than chance. Children thus do appear to understand that decisions should be based on those future actions most likely to achieve their goals.

Nonetheless, Study 2 was intended to test the possibility that children (and adolescents) do not fully understand the normative principle underlying sunk cost decisions. Specifically, we adopted the research approach of Stanovich and West (1999) in their discussion of the "understanding/acceptance principle". According to this principle, the greater the understanding of a decision-making principle, the more likely that normative arguments will be accepted and subsequent decisions will be based on those arguments (see Stanovich & West, 1999, pp. 351 – 352). Alternatively, the less a principle is understood, the more likely that non-normative arguments will be accepted and that subsequent decisions will be based on non-normative heuristics.

Using a variant of the Stanovich and West (1999) methodology, we presented children with arguments for either the normative decision or the non-normative "waste not" (i.e., sunk cost) decision. If children understand the normative principle, but the situational cues that pull for the "waste not" heuristic overwhelm attempts to process information analytically, then arguments for the normative decision should activate this competence (i.e., normative arguments should activate the metacognitive abilities required to override experiential processing). If children understand these arguments and apply them to subsequent decisions, then the case could be made that children do have the requisite competence, but do not apply this competence because they over-rely on heuristics (see Stanovich & West, 1999). Similarly, if children possess the requisite competencies, then they should not be swayed by arguments for the non-normative decision. That is, among those children whose initial decisions are normative, an understanding of the normative principle would be implied if they were not swayed in the non-normative direction by arguments that the "waste not" heuristic is worthwhile.

STUDY 2

Method

Participants. As part of a larger study of children's decision making, 331 9-year-old, ($M = 9.4$ yrs; $SD = .58$; $n = 107$; 50 boys, 57 girls), 12-year-old ($M = 12.3$ yrs; $SD = .44$; $n = 110$; 56 boys, 54 girls), and 15-year-old ($M = 15.6$ yrs; $SD = .61$; $n = 110$; 52 boys, 58 girls) children participated. The 9- and 12-year-olds were drawn from the fourth and seventh grades of two elementary schools that served predominantly mid-SES families. The 15-year-olds were recruited from the tenth grades of the two high schools into which the elementary schools fed. Data from three 9-year-olds were discarded because their teachers reported that these children had serious reading difficulties.

Materials and procedure. For the 9-year-olds, sessions were conducted with groups of no more than four students; modal group size was three. For the 12- and 15 year-olds, groups ranged from three to eight students; at both ages, modal size was four. Sessions lasted between 45 and 60 minutes and were conducted in rooms at participants' schools. Participants were randomly assigned to the conditions described subsequently.

All problems and arguments were presented on separate pages of a 29-page booklet. Although few children had difficulty reading the materials, an undergraduate assistant or teacher was present with each group to answer questions. The instructions, a practice problem (involving the decision to play or read a book, but not involving sunk costs), and a practice argument (again, not involving sunk costs) were read to all participants. Proper use of the rating scales used for the arguments was demonstrated with a large (24 × 12 inch) replica of the scale that appeared in the booklets.

Each session began with a baseline assessment of sunk cost decisions (as well as other types of decisions not discussed here) and, immediately subsequent to this assessment, exposure to normative or non-normative arguments. Two baseline problems were presented. After a brief introduction, children made decisions on both problems. During the second phase, the first problem of the pair was presented again, but children were not asked to make a decision. Instead, an argument that endorsed the normative decision or the non-normative decision for this problem was presented immediately below the problem, and children rated argument strength. The second sunk cost problem was then re-presented with a normative or non-normative argument and rating scale.

In the normative argument (NA) condition, the arguments for both problems were for the normative decision. In the non-normative argument (NN) condition, the two arguments were for the sunk cost decision. In the normative plus non-normative (N + NN) condition, two arguments (one normative, one non-normative) were presented after each problem. In the N + NN condition, the order of the two arguments presented for each problem was counterbalanced. A control condition was included to be identical to the NA and NN conditions, except that descriptions of the characteristics (e.g., tall, outgoing) of the hypothetical decision makers in the problems replaced the arguments.

During the third phase (the "understanding/acceptance" or U/A phase), the problems—but not the arguments—were presented a third time. After being assured that they could make the same or a different decision than they had originally, children again made decisions on each problem. Next, a 5-minute filler task (a simple maze on one page, a hidden picture task on the next page) was given. In the final phase, transfer was assessed on two SC problems the children had not previously seen.

Results

Argument ratings. As an initial step in our analyses, we explored whether ratings of normative and non-normative arguments differed by age and condition. Mean ratings in the three experimental conditions are presented in Table 3. In a first analysis, ratings in the NA condition were compared to ratings in the NN condition. A 3 (age) × 2 (condition) analysis of variance showed that, although ratings were higher in the NA condition than in the NN condition, $F(1, 163) = 18.22$, $p < .001$, this main effect was qualified by an age × condition interaction, $F(2, 163) = 3.74$, $p = .026$. Somewhat surprisingly, follow-up analyses showed both the 9-year-olds ($p < .001$) and the 12-year-olds ($p = .047$) rated normative arguments as superior to non-normative arguments; the 15-year-olds, at least in this between-condition comparison, did not rate normative arguments higher than non-normative arguments. In a second, within-condition analysis, normative argument ratings in the N + NN condition were compared to non-normative argument ratings in the same condition. A 3 (age) × 2 (rating type: normative or non-normative) ANOVA indicated that participants across ages overwhelmingly believed that the normative arguments were superior to the non-normative arguments, $F(1, 76) = 45.26$, $p < .001$. Thus, participants generally rated normative arguments as superior to non-normative arguments. Although the

TABLE 3
Study 2: Mean argument ratings (and SDs) in the experimental conditions

Argument type	NA	NN	N + NN
		Condition	
Normative			
9-year-olds	3.38 (.65)		3.16 (.72)
12-year-olds	3.21 (.74)		3.52 (.66)
15-year-olds	3.04 (.66)		3.29 (.53)
Non-normative			
9-year-olds		2.41 (.81)	2.66 (.75)
12-year-olds		2.76 (.96)	2.30 (.74)
15-year-olds		2.83 (.85)	2.33 (.79)

Ratings could range from 1 to 4.

TABLE 4
Study 2: Mean proportions (and SDs) of normative decisions on the baseline, U/A, and transfer problems

Age	Control	Norm.	Non-norm.	N + NN
		Argument condition		
9 years				
Baseline	.32 (.32)	.25 (.34)	.27 (.36)	.34 (.35)
U/A	.28 (.33)	.38 (.39)	.19 (.29)	.25 (.33)
Transfer	.28 (.38)	.25 (.34)	.23 (.33)	.34 (.31)
12 years				
Baseline	.35 (.33)	.35 (.37)	.34 (.40)	.28 (.35)
U/A	.30 (.32)	.61 (.44)	.19 (.34)	.32 (.44)
Transfer	.35 (.37)	.56 (.31)	.28 (.34)	.35 (.39)
15 years				
Baseline	.44 (.46)	.45 (.40)	.40 (.35)	.43 (.42)
U/A	.38 (.39)	.77 (.31)	.42 (.37)	.67 (.36)
Transfer	.42 (.40)	.82 (.31)	.38 (.41)	.66 (.30)

between-condition analysis indicated that 15-year-olds did not favour one argument type over the other, the within-subjects comparisons showed that, at each age level, normative arguments were considered better than non-normative arguments.

Baseline and understanding/acceptance decisions. Mean proportions of normative responses on the baseline problems are presented in Figure 1 and Table 4. Table 4 also contains means for each condition when the problems were first presented (baseline) and when the same problems were re-presented. An analysis of variance, with age and condition as between-subjects variables and time (baseline, U/A) as a within-subjects variable, revealed significant main effects of age ($p < .001$), and condition ($p = .005$) and significant interactions between age and time, $F(3, 316) = 4.01$, $p = .019$, and condition and time, $F(6, 316) = 11.71$, $p < .001$.

Analyses of the age × time interaction indicated that the effect of time was significant only for the 15-year-olds. The interaction generally arose because age differences were smaller on the baseline problems than on the U/A problems. More importantly, examination of the condition by time interaction indicated that the differences between baseline and U/A scores were not significant in the control and N + NN conditions, scores increased significantly in the NA condition ($p < .001$), and there was a nonsignificant trend for scores to decline in the NN condition ($p = .083$).

However these tests are somewhat misleading because the effects of condition do appear to differ somewhat by age (see Table 4). Thus, to test the hypothesis that even 9-year-olds understand and accept normative arguments, a planned comparison between baseline and U/A scores was conducted separately for each age group. These tests showed that each age group improved from baseline to U/A and, specifically, that the 13% increase in the 9-year-olds' scores was significant, $F(1, 29) = 4.46$, $p = .043$. By contrast, the apparent baseline-to-U/A declines in the NN condition were not significant at any age (smallest $p = .071$, for the 12-year-olds). Finally, in the N + NN condition, the scores of the 15-year-olds, but neither of the younger age groups, improved from baseline to U/A, $F(1, 28) = 7.30$, $p = .012$.

Normative arguments—when presented by themselves—were under-stood, accepted, and applied to subsequent decisions at each age. However, only at 15 years was the persuasive appeal of normative arguments sufficient to overpower that of simultaneously presented non-normative arguments. Although each age rated normative arguments as superior to non-normative arguments, only the 15-year-olds were able to apply their acceptance to subsequent decisions when these competing arguments were presented simultaneously. In general, the results support our suggestion that age differences in sunk cost decisions cannot be entirely explained by failure of children to understand the normative principle.

Sunk cost transfer. Mean transfer scores are presented in Table 4. An age × time (baseline vs transfer) × (condition) analysis of variance yielded significant main effects of age ($p < .001$) and condition ($p = .002$), and significant condition × time, $F(3, 316) = 5.86$, $p = .001$, and age × condition, $F(2, 316) = 2.69$, $p = .015$, interactions. However, although the condition × time interaction gives the appearance that transfer occurred across age groups in the NA condition, in reality this affect arose primarily because of the baseline-to-transfer increases among 12- and 15-year-olds. Indeed, inspection of the 9-year-olds' transfer scores in the NA condition (see Table 4) shows no evidence of transfer whatsoever—that is, scores returned to baseline levels. By contrast, positive transfer was evidenced by the 12- and 15-year-olds in the NA condition, $F(1, 30) = 4.88, p = .035, F(1, 29) = 18.09, p < .001$, respectively, and by the 15-year-olds in the N + NN condition, $F(1, 28) = 4.05, p = .054$.

Correlations among scores and ratings. Partial correlational analyses (controlling for age) indicated, in the experimental conditions, that normative responses at baseline were correlated to normative responses at U/A ($r = .33, p < .001$). However, whereas baseline and transfer scores were unrelated ($r = -.02$), U/A scores were positively related to transfer ($r = .27, p < .001$). Thus, only those participants who accepted and understood the arguments were likely to improve on the transfer problems. Further bolstering this argument are the partial correlations between baseline and transfer scores in the NA and N + NN conditions. Somewhat surprisingly, there was only a modest relationship between normative baseline responses and normative ratings ($r = .15, p = .057$). However, normative ratings were linked to normative decisions both on U/A problems ($r = .38, p < .001$) and on the transfer problems ($r = .23, p = .003$). These correlations were largely unaffected in an additional analysis controlling for normative responses on the baseline problems. Concerning non-normative ratings (in the NN and N + NN conditions), these were negatively, but modestly, linked to baseline ($r = -.15, p = .058$) and U/A ($r = -.16, p = .03$) scores. Non-normative ratings were unrelated to transfer scores, however ($r = .05$). Together, these findings suggest that it was generally only participants who accepted and understood normative arguments and applied these arguments to the U/A problems who evidenced transfer.

Discussion

Study 2 showed, as in Study 1, that despite age-related improvements in sunk cost decisions (on the baseline problems), the responses of most participants were non-normative. Thus, in contrast to the Arkes and Ayton (1999) hypothesis, the tendency to commit the sunk cost fallacy diminishes somewhat with age. In addition, analyses of children's ratings of normative and non-normative arguments indicated that the former were generally treated as superior to the latter. The exception to this finding was that, in the between-condition analysis (but not in the within-subject analysis) contrasting ratings in the NA and NN conditions, the 15-year-olds did not rate the arguments differently. This is surprising because the 15-year-olds' decisions improved considerably in the NA and N + NN conditions and did not decline in the NN condition. Thus, it is perhaps more important to consider the effects of arguments in the N + NN conditions. Across ages in this condition, normative arguments were clearly rated as superior to non-normative arguments.

These findings dovetail nicely with the findings on the U/A problems. When only normative arguments were presented (the NA condition), normative decisions increased for each age group. By contrast, when presented only non-normative arguments (the NN condition), the tendency for normative decisions to decline was not significant. When participants were presented both normative and non-normative arguments, only the U/A decisions of the 15-year-olds were affected. Apparently, the ability to evaluate normative arguments effectively when these arguments compete against intuitively appealing non-normative arguments—and actually *apply* the understanding that emerges from this evaluation—develops only by middle adolescence.

The correlational analyses showed that acceptance of normative arguments improved understanding and application of the normative decision principle (i.e., base decisions on anticipated future consequence rather than on prior investments). Independently of baseline performance and age, children who rated normative arguments highly generally made normative decisions on the U/A problems. By contrast, although a modest tendency was found for children who rated non-normative arguments highly to commit the SC fallacy on the U/A problems, the effect of non-normative arguments was considerably smaller than that of the normative arguments.

Examination of transfer decisions revealed positive transfer in the NA and N + NN conditions. However, these effects were clearly related to age. Only the two adolescent groups evidenced positive transfer in the NA condition and only the 15-year-olds evidenced transfer in the N + NN condition. The latter finding again indicates that only by mid-adolescence does the capacity to simultaneously evaluate and decide between the competing "pulls" of normative and non-normative arguments emerge—at least in the domain of sunk cost decisions (see Klaczynski, in press). Analyses of correlations with baseline scores showed that transfer was unrelated to baseline performance, but was positively associated with normative ratings and normative decisions on the U/A problems. Evidently, transfer was more a function of participants' ability to understand and accept normative arguments than a function of normative decisions made on the baseline problems.

GENERAL DISCUSSION

The results from this work illustrate the general usefulness of applying dual-process theoretic frameworks to developmental phenomena. Specifically, our findings suggest that children, like adults, respond to sunk cost decision situations by initially relying on experientially activated heuristics. Without cues to engage in analytic processing, the particular heuristic we examined— the "waste not" heuristic—is not only automatically activated, but also applied with little or no critical reflection on the appropriateness of the heuristic to particular situations. In general, however, adolescents are somewhat less prone to unreflectively applying the heuristic than children. Our hypothesis is that the increased tendency of adolescents to make normative decisions results from their greater willingness to engage to "metacognitive intercession" (Klaczynski, 2004). Thus, although the "waste not" heuristic is activated automatically for both children and adolescents, it is also momentarily available in working memory for critical scrutiny. However, because they are more likely to have acquired the ability to inhibit such "prepotent" responses, and because they have a better understanding that simply because a decision strategy is activated it does not need to be applied, adolescents are more disposed to evaluating heuristics before actually implementing them.

Results from Study 2 provide further support for this argument. Specifically, the greater difficulties children have with sunk cost decisions do not appear to arise because they lack the analytic competence to understand the normative principle. Across ages, normative arguments were rated as superior to non-normative arguments; across ages, decisions improved from baseline performance when the problems were re-presented after normative arguments had been evaluated. Thus, at least some minimal level of decision competence was available even at 9 years of age. The critical differences between children and adolescents were found on the transfer problems. Here, only adolescents applied the general understanding of the normative principle they had gleaned from the arguments to problems for which the arguments were not directly intended.

Again, this age difference can be attributed to metacognitive differences between children and adolescents. Children were apparently limited in their argument evaluation capacities such that they could apply their under-standing of the arguments only to the original problems. Because of an increased capacity to abstract domain-general decision rules from the normative arguments and determine the appropriateness of these rules to novel problems, adolescents performed better than children on the transfer problems.

When children were presented both normative and non-normative arguments after making baseline decisions (i.e., the N + NN condition), a second "level" of age-related difference was found. That is, despite the fact the children at each age (in the within-subjects analyses) rated the normative arguments as superior, only the 15-year-olds were able to apply their understanding of the arguments to the U/A and transfer problems. This suggests that the interference created by logically irrelevant arguments prevents children and early adolescents from applying their understanding of normative arguments to subsequent decisions. Developments in the capacity to inhibit such interference (see Reyna & Brainerd, 1995) continue after the onset of adolescence and perhaps into adulthood. Prior to mid-adolescence, children seem capable of pulling apart and distinguishing between simultaneously presented normative and non-normative arguments. However, children seem to be incapable of proceeding to the next step—applying what they gleaned from these arguments to subsequent decisions. Additional work on developmental trends in the capacity to inhibit interference, particularly during adolescence, is required to flush this possibility out more completely. Nonetheless, our data provide suggestive evidence that the metacognitive abilities to evaluate both types of argument, and perhaps the working memory capacity that affords the ability to evaluate competing strategies for subsequent decisions, emerges relatively late in development.

Conclusions

In contrast to cognitive and social psychology, dual-process theories have had relatively short lives in developmental psychology. Because a consider-able amount of developmental research has been devoted to age-related changes in analytic processing, particularly important for future research are more precise investigations of the relationships among age, inhibition abilities, and experiential processing. Little is currently known of the "ifs" and "hows" of experiential processing changes with age. Similarly, age-related changes in the mechanisms regulating interactions between experi-ential and analytic processing have not been thoroughly explored. Regarding these interactions, we suggest that experientially activated heuristics are—for children, adolescents, and adults—at least momentarily available in working memory before they are applied. While in working memory, heuristics may be evaluated for their appropriateness to particular situations.

In situations in which people have few or no personal investments (e.g., the outcome of a decision is, at least subjectively, unlikely to negatively impact important personal goals) or in which there is little time for reflective contemplation, heuristics are likely to be employed automatically. However, given adequate time and motivation to evaluate heuristics, the potential for pre-application evaluation exists for children, adolescents, and adults. With development, such metacognitive and executive function skills as the abilities to evaluate and justify strategies (see Moshman, 1998) and to inhibit prepotent responses emerge. Even by adulthood, however, these skills are far from completely developed (Kuhn, 2000, 2001; Kuhn et al., 1988; Moshman, 1998).

A dual-process approach to development complements and extends "competence/performance" theories of development (e.g., Overton, 1985). Specifically, competence/performance views attempt to distinguish between underlying analytic competencies and situational factors that interfere with the ability to apply these competencies. However, such theories have not focused explicitly on the mechanisms and outcomes of processing when logically relevant competencies are not activated. That is, reasoning and decisions are "written off" to such performance factors as impulsivity and unfamiliarity (and, at times, to familiarity) without sufficient attention to precisely how these factors affect performance. A dual-process view focuses on three aspects of processing not typically accounted for in competence/performance theories.

First, dual-process theories call attention to the role of "metacognitive intercession," and failures to engage in such intercession effectively. This theorising is consistent with cognitive theorists' (e.g., Evans & Over, 1996; Stanovich, 1999) claims that, although experiential processing is the default processing system, this processing can be overridden by analytic processing. The process of overriding experiential processing predominance, however, would seem to require advanced metacognitive and executive function abilities, as well as the types of thinking dispositions discussed by Baron (1985, 1988), Perkins, Jay, and Tishman (1993), and Stanovich and West (1998, 2000; Stanovich, 1999; see also Kokis et al., 2002).

Second, dual-process accounts provide explicit descriptions of the mechanisms that guide performance when the analytic system is not predominant. Thus, for example, when analytic competencies are not predominant, performance appears to depend largely on memory-based strategies and heuristics that are automatically activated and applied. Third, and relatedly, dual-process accounts do not operate on the assumption that experientially guided performance is necessarily irrational. Instead, under most conditions, the outcomes of experiential processing are beneficial or, at least, not harmful. Without the speed with which a wide array of information is processed experientially, real-world functioning would be impossible. Similarly, if not for the rapidity and automaticity afforded by experiential processing, information processing would be over-taxed; again, it would not be possible for explicit learning and reasoning to occur.

Although dual-process theories have emerged to explain age-related developments in implicit and explicit memory (see Brainerd & Reyna, 2001; Schneider & Bjorklund, 1998), similar developmental accounts of reasoning and decision making have been slower to take hold. Developmental memory researchers (e.g., Guttentag & Dunn, 2003) have increasingly recognised that implicit memory interacts with conscious strategy use to determine performance. Likewise, developmental research on reasoning would profit from further theoretical and empirical distinctions between implicit and explicit processing and additional attention to developments in both processing systems.

REFERENCES

Arkes, H. R., & Ayton, P. (1999). The sunk cost and concorde effects: Are humans less rational than animals? *Psychological Review, 125*, 591–600.

Bargh, J. A., & Chartland, T. L. (1999). The unbearable automaticity of being. *American Psychologist, 54*, 462–479.

Baron, J. (1985). *Rationality and intelligence.* Cambridge, MA: Cambridge University Press.

Baron, J. (1988). *Thinking and deciding.* New York: Cambridge.

Baron, J., Granato, L., Spranca, M., & Teubal, E. (1993). Decision-making biases in children and early adolescence: Exploratory studies. *Merrill-Palmer Quarterly, 39*, 22–46.

Birch, L., Fisher, J., & Grimm-Thomas, K. (1999). Children and food. In M. Siegal & C. Petersen (Eds.), *Children's understanding of biology and health* (pp. 161–182). New York: Cambridge University Press.

Brainerd, C. J., & Reyna, V. A. (2001). Fuzzy-trace theory: Dual processes in memory, reasoning, and cognitive neuroscience. In H. W. Reese & R., Kail (Eds.), *Advances in children development and behavior* (Vol. 28, pp. 41–100). San Diego: Academic Press.

Byrnes, J. P. (1998). *The nature and development of decision making: A self-regulation model.* Hillsdale, NJ: Lawrence Erlbaum Associates Inc.

Case, R. (1985). *Intellectual development: Birth to adulthood.* New York: Academic Press.

Case, R. (1998). The development of conceptual structures. In W. Damon (Series Ed.) & D. Kuhn & R. Siegler (Vol. Eds.), *Handbook of child psychology: Vol. 2. Cognition, perception, and language* (5th ed., pp. 745–800). New York: Wiley.

Davidson, D. (1995). The representativeness heuristic and the conjunction fallacy in children's decision making. *Merrill-Palmer Quarterly, 41*, 328–346.

Donaldson, M. (1978). *Children's minds.* London: Fontana.

Epstein, S. (1994). Integration of the cognitive and psychodynamic unconscious. *American Psychologist, 49*, 709–724.

Epstein, S., & Pacini, R. (1999). Some basic issues regarding dual-process theories from the perspective of cognitive-experiential self-theory. In S. Chaiken & Y. Trope (Eds.), *Dual-process theories in social psychology* (pp. 462–482). New York: Guilford Press.

Evans, J. St. B. T. (1989). *Bias in human reasoning: Causes and consequences.* Hove, UK: Lawrence Erlbaum Associates Ltd.

Evans, J. St. B. T. (2002). Logic and human reasoning: An assessment of the deduction paradigm. *Psychological Bulletin, 128*, 978–996.

Evans, J. St. B. T., & Over, D. E. (1996). *Reasoning and rationality.* Hove, UK: Psychology Press.

Gigerenzer, G. (1996). On narrow norms and vague heuristics: A reply to Kahneman and Tversky. *Psychological Review, 103*, 592–596.

Gopnick, A., & Wellman, H. M. (1994). The theory theory. In L. A. Hirshfield & S. A. Gelman (Eds.), *Mapping the mind: Domain specificity in cognition and culture* (pp. 391–411). New York: Cambridge University Press.

Guttentag. R., & Dunn, J. (2003). Judgments of remembering: The revelation effect in children and adults. *Journal of Experimental Child Psychology, 86*, 153–167.

Heath, C. (1995). Escalation and de-escalation of commitment to sunk costs: The role of budgeting in mental accounting. *Organizational Behavior and Human Decision Processes, 62*, 38–54.

Inhelder, B., & Piaget, J. (1958). *The growth of logical thinking from childhood to adolescence.* New York: Basic.

Jacobs, J. E., & Ganzel, A. K. (1993). Decision-making in adolescence: Are we asking the wrong question? *Advances in Motivation and Achievement, 8*, 1–31.

Jacobs, J. E., & Potenza, M. (1991). The use of judgment heuristics to make social and object decisions: A developmental perspective. *Child Development, 62*, 166–178.

Klaczynski, P. A. (2000). Motivated scientific reasoning biases, epistemological beliefs, and theory polarization: A two-process approach to adolescent cognition. *Child Development, 71*, 1347–1366.

Klaczynski, P. A. (2001a). Analytic and heuristic processing influences on adolescent reasoning and decision making. *Child Development, 72*, 844–861.

Klaczynski, P. A. (2001b). Framing effects on adolescent task representations, analytic and heuristic processing, and decision making: Implications for the normative-descriptive gap. *Journal of Applied Developmental Psychology, 22*, 289–309.

Klaczynski, P. A. (2004). A dual-process model of adolescent development: Implications for decision making, reasoning, and identity. In R. Kail (Ed.), *Advances in child development and behavior* (Vol. 31). New York: Academic Press.

Klaczynski, P. A. (in press). Metacognition and cognitive variability: A dual-process model of decision making and its development. In J. E. Jacobs & P. A. Klaczynski (Eds.), *The development of decision making*. Mahwah, NJ: Lawrence Erlbaum Associates Inc.

Klaczynski, P. A., & Narasimham, G. (1998). Problem representations as mediators of adolescent deductive reasoning. *Developmental Psychology, 34*, 865–881.

Kokis, J. V., Macpherson, R., Toplak, M. E., West, R. F., & Stanovich, K. E. (2002). Heuristic and analytic processing: Age trends and associations with cognitive ability and cognitive styles. *Journal of Experimental Child Psychology, 83*, 26–52.

Krouse, H. J. (1986). Use of decision frames by elementary school children. *Perceptual and Motor Skills, 63*, 1107–1112.

Kuhn, D. (2000). Metacognitive development. *Current Directions in Psychological Science, 9*, 178–181.

Kuhn, D. (2001). How do people know? *Psychological Science, 12*, 1–8.

Kuhn, D., Amsel, E., & O'Loughlin, M. (1988). *The development of scientific thinking skills*. Orlando, FL: Academic Press.

Lie, E., & Newcombe, N. S. (1999). Elementary school children's explicit and implicit memory for faces of preschool classmates. *Developmental Psychology, 35*, 102–112.

Markovits, H., & Barrouillet, P. (2002). The development of conditional reasoning: A mental model account. *Developmental Review, 22*, 5–36.

Markovits, H., & Dumas, C. (1999). Developmental patterns of understanding social and physical transitivity. *Journal of Experimental Child Psychology, 73*, 95–114.

McCarthy, A. M., Schoorman, F. D., & Cooper, A. C. (1993). Reinvestment decisions by entrepreneurs: Rational decision-making or escalation of commitment? *Journal of Business, 8*, 9–24.

Moshman, D. (1990). The development of metalogical understanding. In W. F. Overton (Ed.), *Reasoning, necessity, and logic: Developmental perspectives* (pp. 205–225). Hillsdale, NJ: Lawrence Erlbaum Associates Inc.

Moshman, D. (1998). Cognitive development beyond childhood. In W. Damon (Series Ed.) & D. Kuhn & R. Siegler (Vol. Eds.), *Handbook of child psychology: Vol. 2. Cognition, perception, and language* (5th ed., pp. 745–800). New York: Wiley.

Moshman, D. (1999). *Adolescent psychological development*. Mahwah, NJ: Lawrence Erlbaum Associates Inc.

Overton, W. F. (1985). Scientific methodologies and the competence-moderator-performance issue. In E. Neimark, R. DeLisi, & J. Newman (Eds.), *Moderators of performance* (pp. 15–41) Hillsdale, NJ: Lawrence Erlbaum Associates Inc.

Overton, W. F. (1990). Competence and procedures: Constraints on the development of logical reasoning. In W. F. Overton (Ed.), *Reasoning, necessity, and logic: Developmental perspectives* (pp. 1–32). Hillsdale, NJ: Lawrence Erlbaum Associates Inc.

Perkins, D. N., Jay, E., & Tishman, S. (1993). Beyond abilities: A dispositional theory of thinking. *Merrill-Palmer Quarterly, 39*, 1–21.

Piaget, J. (1972). Intellectual evolution from adolescence to adulthood. *Human Development, 15*, 1–12.

Reber, A. S. (1992). An evolutionary contexts for the cognitive unconscious. *Philosophical Psychology, 5*, 33–51.

Reyna, V. F., & Brainerd, C. J. (1995). Fuzzy-trace theory: An interim synthesis. *Learning and Individual Differences, 7*, 1–75.

Reyna, V. F., & Ellis, S. C. (1994). Fuzzy-trace theory and framing effects in children's risky decision making. *Psychological Science, 5*, 275–279.

Ruffman, T., Perner, J., Olson, D. R., & Doherty, M. (1993). Reflecting on scientific thinking: Children's understanding of the hypothesis–evidence relation. *Child Development, 64*, 1617–1636.

Schneider, W., & Bjorklund, D. F. (1998). Memory. In W. Damon (Series Ed.) & D. Kuhn & R. Siegler (Vol. Eds.), *Handbook of child psychology: Vol. 2. Cognition, perception, and language* (5th ed., pp. 745–800). New York: Wiley.

Stanovich, K. E. (1999). *Who is rational? Studies of individual differences in reasoning.* Mahwah, NJ: Lawrence Erlbaum Associates Inc.

Stanovich, K. E., & West, R. F. (1997). Reasoning independently of prior belief and individual differences in actively open-minded thinking. *Journal of Educational Psychology, 89*, 342–357.

Stanovich, K. E., & West, R. F. (1998). Individual differences in rational thought. *Journal of Experimental Psychology: General, 127*, 161–188.

Stanovich, K. E., & West, R. F. (1999). Discrepancies between normative and descriptive models of decision making and the understanding/acceptance principle. *Cognitive Psychology, 38*, 349–385.

Stanovich, K. E., & West, R. F. (2000). Individual differences in reasoning: Implications for the rationality debate? *Behavioral and Brain Sciences, 23*, 645–665.

Staw, B. M. (1976). Knee-deep in the big muddy: A study of escalating commitment to a chosen course of action. *Organizational Behavior and Human Performance, 16*, 27–44.

Steinberg, L., & Cauffman, E. (1996). Maturity of judgment in adolescence: Psychosocial factors in adolescent decision-making. *Law and Human Behavior, 20*, 249–272.

Wason, P. C. (1966). Reasoning. In B. Foss (Ed.), *New horizons in psychology.* Harmondsworth, UK: Penguin Books.

Webley, P., & Plaiser, Z. (1998). Mental accounting in childhood. *Children's Social and Economic Education, 3*, 55–64.

Wellman, H., & Gelman, S. A. (1992). Cognitive development: Foundational theories for core domains. *Annual Review of Psychology, 43*, 337–375.

APPENDIX A

Monetary SC decision

Tom had $20 to buy a ticket to see a clown at the carnival. There are two clowns who have shows, Howlin' Hank and Laughin' Larry. Because the two shows are at the same time, Tom could only buy a ticket to see one clown. Tom has always wanted to see Howlin' Hank because everybody says he's so funny. So, he spent all of his money and bought a ticket for Howlin' Hank.

Then, Tom found out that he had bought the *wrong ticket*! His ticket was really for Laughin' Larry. All of Tom's friends have said that Laughin' Larry isn't nearly as funny as Howlin' Hank. But the people who sold Tom the ticket said that he could not have his money back. Tom was very upset that he wouldn't be able to see Howlin' Hank.

Then, Tom checked his pocket. To his surprise, Tom found that he had more money. If fact, he still had $20—if he wanted to, he could buy the right ticket and still see the show with Howlin' Hank.

What should Tom do?

Spend another $20 and buy a ticket to see Howlin' Hank

Use the ticket he already bought to see Laughin' Larry

Time/effort SC decision

On parents' day at Julie's school, there will be a contest where all the students' paintings will be shown. Julie has spent the last 14 days working really hard on a drawing. She wants to win a prize pretty badly and thinks her drawing has a chance to win. Now, at long last, the drawing is almost finished.

Then, just four days before the contest, Julie had an idea for a totally different drawing. She is positive that she could draw the new picture in four days, just in time for the contest. Not only that, but Julie thinks that the new drawing would be a lot better than the one she's been working on. The problem is that Julie has only one drawing board. That means that if she wants to draw the new picture, she will have to completely erase the picture she's been working on.

What should Julie do?

Erase the old picture and draw the new one

Keep the drawing she's been working on

Monetary N-SC decision

Tom has $20 to buy a ticket to see a clown at the carnival. There are two clowns who have shows, Howlin' Hank and Laughin' Larry. Because the two shows are at the same time, Tom can only buy a ticket to see one clown. Tom has always wanted to see Howlin' Hank because everybody says he's so funny. Then, he found out that a ticket for Howlin' Hank cost $40—and Tom only had $20. Tom was very upset that he wouldn't be able to see Howlin' Hank.

All of Tom's friends have said that Laughin' Larry isn't as nearly funny as Howlin' Hank. However, Tom could see Laughin' Larry because tickets for Laughin' only cost $20.

Then, when he was standing in line to buy a ticket for Laughin' Larry, Tom checked his pocket. To his surprise, Tom found that he more money than he thought—he actually had $40! If he wanted to, he could buy a ticket for the show with Howlin' Hank.

What should Tom do?

Spent $40 for a ticket to see Howlin' Hank

Spend $20 for a ticket to see Laughin' Larry

Time/effort N-SC decision

On parents' day, there will be a contest at Julie's school where all the students' drawings will be shown. When Julie came up with an idea for a drawing, she thought that it could be really good if she worked really hard on it for the next two weeks. Julie wants to win a prize pretty badly and thinks her idea for a drawing would have a chance to win.

Before she started working on the drawing, Julie had an idea for a totally different drawing that would take her about 18 days to finish if she worked really hard. Julie thinks this picture will be even better than the one she would create with her first idea. The problem is that Julie has only one drawing board. That means that she will be able to draw only the first picture or only the second picture.

What should Julie do?

Work on the second idea she had for a drawing

Work on the first idea she had for a drawing

APPENDIX B

Sunk cost arguments

Remember, Julie spent 3 weeks working on a very good drawing for the contest. But then, just 2 days before the contest, she came up with another idea for a drawing. She thinks that the new drawing will be better than the one she worked on for 3 weeks. The problem is that, in order to draw the new picture, she will have to throw out the old picture.

So, she asked Amy (or Tara) for her advice.

Normative. Amy thinks that Julie should erase the old picture and draw the new one because:

All the time that Julie put into the old picture doesn't make any difference. She wants to win, so she should use the new picture. She shouldn't worry about what she's already done. The work she put into the old one is in the past—she can't let that affect her now. Because she really wants to win, she's got to go with the best picture, even if she has to throw out a picture she worked hard on.

Non-normative. Tara thinks that Julie should keep working on the picture that she's spent three weeks on because:

Julie's worked on this picture for 3 weeks. Even if the new picture would be better, all of her imagination and effort were in the old picture. She should show a picture that really means something to her. She worked really hard on that picture. If she doesn't use the one she worked so hard on, all of that time and effort will be wasted. If she doesn't use the old picture, she'll just be throwing away three weeks of work.

THINKING & REASONING, 2004, *10* (2), 175–195

Working memory, inhibitory control and the development of children's reasoning

Simon J. Handley, A. Capon, M. Beveridge, I. Dennis, and
J. St. B. T. Evans

University of Plymouth, UK

The ability to reason independently from one's own goals or beliefs has long been recognised as a key characteristic of the development of formal operational thought. In this article we present the results of a study that examined the correlates of this ability in a group of 10-year-old children ($N = 61$). Participants were presented with conditional and relational reasoning items, where the content was manipulated such that the conclusion to the arguments were either congruent, neutral, or incongruent with beliefs, and either logically valid or logically invalid. Participants also received a measure of working memory capacity (the counting span task) and a measure of inhibitory control (the stop signal task). Indices of belief bias and logical reasoning on belief-based problems were predicted independently by both measures. In contrast logical reasoning on belief neutral problems was predicted by working memory alone. The findings suggest that executive functions play a key role in the development of children's ability to decontextualise their thinking.

An aspect of reasoning that is receiving increasing attention in both the adult and developmental literatures is the extent to which beliefs mediate logical performance on deductive reasoning tasks (see, for example, Dias & Harris, 1988; 1990; Leevers & Harris, 1999). According to a number of theorists a hallmark of formal reasoning competence is the ability to decontextualise, or reason logically from premises irrespective of their content (Moshman & Franks, 1986). Indeed the ability to recognise that validity is a function of an argument's form rather than its empirical status is viewed as a characteristic of the transition from a stage in which children possess an implicit understanding of logic to one in which this understanding becomes accessible to awareness (Moshman, 1990). This transition

---

Correspondence should be addressed to Dr S. J. Handley, Centre for Thinking and Language, Department of Psychology, University of Plymouth, Plymouth, Devon, UK. Email: shandley@plymouth.ac.uk

© 2004 Psychology Press Ltd

http://www.tandf.co.uk/journals/pp/13546783.html   DOI: 10.1080/13546780442000051

is proposed to occur at around 10 to 12 years of age, at the same point at which children begin to reliably distinguish between logical and non-logical argument forms, in the absence of contextual support (Markovits, Scheifler & Fortier, 1989).

The ability to reason independent of one's own beliefs is widely viewed as a core cognitive ability that underlies the development of critical and analytic thinking skills (see, for example, Klacynski, Gordon & Fauth, 1997; Pithers & Soden, 2000). Although the developmental changes that occur in reasoning performance of this kind are well documented, surprisingly little is known concerning how or why such transitions occur and the ways in which other cognitive factors influence the development of these abilities.

In contrast, in the adult literature researchers have begun to examine the correlates of reasoning performance, in particular on tasks in which logic and beliefs dictate different responses (see for example, Stanovich, 1999). Two aspects of cognitive processing consistently predict reasoning performance, cognitive ability and thinking style (Stanovich, 1999). Cognitive ability is assumed to reflect the capacity of an explicit processing or working memory system, whilst thinking style is a personality-based measure that reflects such things as openness to ideas, considerations of alternatives, and cognitive flexibility. The adult work is generally grounded in theoretical accounts that emphasise the distinction between explicit processes, which are conscious, effortful, and limited by cognitive capacity, and implicit processes, which are pre-conscious, automatic, and not capacity-limited (see, for example, Evans & Over, 1996; Stanovich, 1999). In most of these accounts the explicit system is linked to deductive reasoning, novel problem solving, and intelligence, whilst the implicit system is associated with belief-based, pragmatic, language-based processes. On this analysis belief-based responses are viewed as automatic default processes that may be overridden by the explicit system given sufficient processing resources. To illustrate, consider you are given the following argument and asked to judge the logical validity of the conclusion:

People are bigger than elephants

Elephants are bigger than houses

Therefore houses are bigger than people

According to a dual process account the implicit belief-based system will cue reasoners towards accepting the conclusion. In order to perform accurately on such problems, this response must be resisted and a full logical analysis completed. According to Stanovich (1999, see also, Evans & Over, 1996), the ability to resist belief-based responding is highly dependent on the cognitive resources of the explicit system. The greater the resources available, the more adept a reasoner is at resisting beliefs and giving normative responses.

The functions associated with the explicit system under these accounts bear close resemblance to those functions associated with an executive or supervisory attentional system. Executive functions are those processes that enable us to engage in novel problem solving and purposeful goal-directed behaviour (see, for example, Rabbitt, 1997). These may involve constructing and holding in mind a mental representation of a given task, the generation of a strategic plan of action sequences, and the ability to inhibit task-irrelevant processes, or defer responses to a more appropriate time (see, for example, Miyake & Shah, 1999; Welsh & Pennington, 1988). The concept of executive function is strongly associated with the idea of a limited-capacity central processing system. These supervisory or executive processes are implicated in many forms of complex behaviour including novel problem solving, reasoning, and much of human social behaviour (Pennington & Ozonoff, 1996).

Hence one set of candidate processes that are likely to influence the course of reasoning development are those processes associated with executive function. Most contemporary accounts of reasoning invoke executive processing constraints to explain both individual differences in adult reasoning and developmental transitions in children's reasoning (see, for example, Johnson-Laird & Byrne, 1991; Markovits, 2000). There is also a suggestion from neuro-imaging research that inhibitory processes may be invoked on reasoning problems that require a response that is contrary to beliefs (Goel, Buchel, Frith & Dolan, 2000). Similarly in the neuropsychological literature executive processes are commonly assumed to play a role in the control of a range of cognitive processes including deductive reasoning and problem solving (see, for example, Baddeley, 1986; Burgess, 1997).

Whilst the impact of various developmental psychopathologies, such as attention deficit hyperactivity disorder (ADHD) and autism, on executive function tasks is an area of increasing research interest (see, for a review, Pennington & Ozonoff, 1996), there is surprisingly little known about the relationship between executive function and reasoning development. Indeed, as yet, research examining the role of inhibitory control and executive capacity in reasoning has not been extended into the developmental domain.

In the present paper we examine the relationship between belief-based reasoning, working memory, and inhibitory control. In the study that follows we examine children's reasoning on problems of the kind shown above, where the believability of the conclusion and its logical status are systematically manipulated. As we shall see this enables us to generate a range of indices reflecting a child's logical ability and the extent to which beliefs bias their reasoning.

In addition we administered a measure of working memory capacity (the counting span task) and a measure of inhibition (the stop signal task). Theoretical accounts of reasoning invariably invoke working memory constraints as a limiter of reasoning success. The ability to integrate and manipulate premise information is considered to draw on a working memory system that enables the simultaneous representation and manipulation of information. Hence we expect variations in working memory to be predictive of logical reasoning performance. In addition, however, problems of the kind shown above also require reasoners to resist a response based on their own beliefs and to focus on the logical structure of an argument rather than its empirical status. Resisting pre-potent responses is a characteristic commonly associated with executive control or inhibition, and hence we might expect variations in this ability, as measured by the stop signal task, to be predictive of performance on problems in which there is a belief component.

METHOD

Participants

The participants were 61 school children recruited from two primary schools in the City of Plymouth. The sample consisted of 39 girls and 22 boys, with a mean age of 121 months (min 110 months, max 133 months). Both schools received goodwill payments for participating in the study.

Materials and procedure

Participants completed the tasks during two testing sessions, each lasting approximately 20 minutes. The participants were tested individually. Session 1 consisted of the stop signal task and a relational reasoning task. Session 2 consisted of a working memory task and a conditional reasoning task. All participants carried out these tasks in the same order.

Inhibition task: The stop signal task. The stop signal task is a computerised measure of inhibitory control that is based on a formal theory of inhibition (see Logan, Cowan, & Davis, 1984). Whilst a range of task variants have been developed in this study we employed a version based on one used by Aman, Roberts, and Pennington (1998). The task was selected because performance on it has consistently been shown to differentiate between typically developing children and children with attention deficit disorder (see, for example, Nigg, 1999). Given that children with ADD are characterised as having a specific deficit in inhibitory control, the poorer performance of ADD children on this task suggests that the measure is tapping into the construct of inhibition.

The stop signal task consists of two types of trial; primary task trials and stop signal trials. On primary task trials a fixation point (a small smiley face) was presented on the screen for 500 ms followed by the presentation of an X or an O. The child responded by pressing an X button or an O button on one of two button boxes. On stop signal trials the X or the O is presented along with a tone or stop signal. On these trials the child is instructed to withhold their response. The tones were presented randomly at 150 ms or 250 ms before the child's mean reaction time (MRT) to primary trials. Because the tone delay is set relative to the MRT for each child, the inhibitory demands are independent of the response time to primary trials and approximately equivalent for each participant.

The children completed four blocks of trials. The first block consisted of 30 primary task trials (15 of X and 15 of O). These trials familiarised the child with task while establishing the MRT that was used for setting the tone delays for subsequent blocks of trials. The second block consisted of 24 practice trials in which 16 primary trials and 8 stop signal trials (two at each delay). The remaining two blocks of 48 trials were the experimental blocks. Each block consisted of 32 primary trials and 16 stop signal trials (8 at each delay) randomly interspersed with the primary trials. The fixation point appeared first on the screen for 500 ms, followed by the presentation of either an O or an X for a further 1000 ms. A blank screen was then presented for 500 ms followed by the next fixation point. Children received the following set of instructions prior to the first block of trials:

> In this part of the game the computer will show a smiley face in the middle of the screen. You need to look at the smiley face as it acts as a target for you to watch. Then the computer will show either the letter O or the letter X. If you see the letter O come up on the screen, then you should press the button marked O. If you see the letter X come up on the screen, then you should press the button marked X. You should try and do this as fast as you can. If you make any mistakes—do not worry and just carry on. Do you understand what you have to do? OK—get ready for the smiley face.

and received the following additional instructions prior to the second block of trials:

> The next part of the game is a bit different. You will still see either the letter O or the letter X come up on the screen. BUT, sometimes you will also hear a beep. Let's listen to the beep now! When you hear the beep you should try NOT to press the O or X buttons. When you do not hear a beep, you should press the O and X buttons just as you did in the first part of the game. Again do not worry if you make any mistakes—just keep going. Do you understand what you have to do? OK—get ready for the smiley face.

The main measure of performance on the task was accuracy on the stop signal trials (max = 32). Independent measures of accuracy at each of the stop signal delays were also recorded (max = 16).

Relational and conditional reasoning tasks.   The reasoning problems that were used in the study were drawn from research on the development of children's reasoning (Evans & Perry, 1995; Moshman & Franks, 1986). Children received a total of 24 reasoning problems: 12 based on transitive relations and 12 based on conditional relations. The conditional reasoning problems and the relational reasoning problems took one of four logical forms as shown in Table 1.

The Determinate-Yes arguments are ones in which the conclusion is logically determined by the premises and the correct response is Yes. The Determinate-No arguments are ones in which the conclusion is logically falsified by the premises and the correct response is No. The indeterminate problems are ones in which the conclusion is neither determined nor falsified by the conclusion and the correct response is to indicate that it is not possible to tell whether the conclusion follows.

Each logical form of the arguments was paired with a believable, a neutral/arbitrary, or an unbelievable conclusion. The conclusions to the conditional items had been rated in a previous study with respect to their believability amongst a group of 10- and 11-year-old children (Evans &

TABLE 1
The logical structure of the reasoning problems

Conditional problems	
Determinate Yes (DY)	Determinate No (DN)
P → Q	P · Q
Q · R	Q · not-R
P · R	P · R
Indeterminate 1	Indeterminate 2
P · Q	P · Q
R · Q	not-R · Q
P · R	P · R

Relational problems	
Determinate Yes (DY)	Determinate No (DN)
P · Q	P · Q
Q · R	Q · R
P · R	R · P
Indeterminate 1	Indeterminate 2
P · Q	Q · P
R · Q	Q · R
P · R	R · P

Each argument consists of two premises followed by a conclusion. P · Q means P implies Q for the conditional problems, and indicates that a transitive relationship holds between P and Q for the relational problems.

Perry, 1995). The conclusions to the relational items could be objectively classified as believable or unbelievable as a function of the relative size of known objects (see Appendix). The neutral relational problems contained arbitrary content and the neutral conditional items were ones in which the conclusion had been pre-rated in a previous study as neither believable nor unbelievable. The full set of problems is presented in the Appendix.

Children were instructed in the task in the following way:

Today I am here to test you on a short task. You will be shown some sentences on some cards. Some of these sentences might sound a bit funny or strange, but I want you to play the game that they are all true, and think about what things would be like if they were true. The question I ask will be about what you think follows from the sentences. There will be three answers to choose from and I want you to tell me which one of the answers you think is right. If you think that it is not possible to tell which is the right answer, then you must say so.

Everything I say is written down in front of you so you can read it as many times as you want. If you want me to repeat anything I say you can ask me and if you want me to stop at any point you can do so and I won't mind. Shall we carry on? Lets try some together, and remember, the sentences might sound funny but I want you to imagine that everything I tell you is true.

The problems were presented on cards and consisted of two simple practice items followed by the experimental items of the following kind. Examples of a relational and a conditional problem are shown below:

Transitive reasoning problem

Insects are smaller than mice

Mice are smaller than rabbits

Imagining the two sentences above are true, does it follow that

Rabbits are smaller then insects?

Conditional reasoning problem

Cars run on petrol

All things that run on petrol carry people

Imagining the two sentences above are true, does it follow that

Cars carry people?

Following the presentation of each problem, children were presented with a choice of the following three response options:

YES

NO

It is not possible to tell

The child gave a verbal response and this was recorded on a response sheet. Four main indices of performance were calculated on the task. The *belief index* reflected the number of responses that were consonant with believability of the conclusion. A point was awarded for the acceptance of a believable conclusion and the rejection of an unbelievable conclusion, irrespective of the logical structure of the problem. This measure was based on performance on the 16 problems in which the conclusion was either believable or unbelievable. The *logic thematic index* was a measure of logical performance on the same problems, where a point was awarded for correct acceptance of a logically valid conclusion, the rejection of a logically false conclusion, and an impossible to tell response to indeterminate problems. The maximum score on this measure was 16. The *conflict index* was a measure of logical performance on those problems in which there was direct conflict between the logical response and the belief-based response. The maximum score on this index was 4. Finally the *logic neutral index* reflected logical accuracy on those problems with a belief neutral or arbitrary conclusion. The maximum score on this index was 8.

Working memory task: The counting span

The counting span task was modelled on a measure developed by Case, Kurland, and Goldberg (1982). The task consists of a processing component that requires counting the number of coloured dots present on a computer screen and a storage component that involves the storage of the products of a series of these counting operations. The child was presented with a series of cards on a computer screen, each card showing a number of blue and red coloured dots in a randomly determined irregular pattern. The child's task was to count out loud the number of red dots from each card. The child received a practice set of two cards followed by three trials consisting of two cards, three trials of three cards, three trials of four cards, and three trials of five cards. All children worked through all of these trials, regardless of performance. Participants were instructed on the task in the following way:

> This game is called the counting game! This is a game about counting and remembering RED dots! On the next screen will be a set of blue and red dots. You must count just the RED dots by pointing at each one and counting them up out loud. You need to REMEMBER how many RED dots you've counted! Then another screen will appear with more blue and red dots. Again, you must count the RED dots by pointing at each one and counting them up out loud and again, you need to REMEMBER how many RED dots you've counted! After this you need to tell me how many RED dots you counted on the FIRST screen followed by how many RED dots you counted on the SECOND screen. So, it is a game about remembering sets of red dots that you've seen previously. At the start of the game you will only have to remember two sets of red dots in a row. But, as the game goes on you will need to remember three, four and five sets of red dots. Do you

understand what you have to do? If so, shall we have a go at a couple of practice sets?

A working memory span score was calculated in the following way. If a child was correct on two out of three trials at a certain level, then they were assigned a span score at that level. For example if a child answered at least two of the three trials at set level 3 correctly then they were awarded a span score of 3. If, however, they then went on to correctly identify one more set at the next set level up, then their score was incremented by .5. The maximum span score on the task was 5.

RESULTS

Table 2 presents the descriptive data for the reasoning, working memory, and stop signal tasks. As Table 2 shows most of the measures showed a reasonable range and degree of variance.

The reliability of each of the measures was also calculated. The reliability of the working memory span task was calculated by performing a split-half correlation between odd and even trials within each set level. The Spearman-Brown formula was then used to provide an estimate of reliability for this task. As Table 2 shows, the working memory span produced a corrected correlation of over $r = .50$, a satisfactory level of reliability for group measurement (Rust & Golombok, 1999). The reliability of the remaining measures was calculated using Cronbach's Alpha, treating each stop signal trial or reasoning problem that contributed to the score on a measure as an individual item. The reliabilities of the reasoning indices were all at an acceptable level (alpha range = .57 to .85). The reliabilities of the overall

TABLE 2
Descriptive statistics for the reasoning, counting span and stop signal tasks

	Mean	Min	Max	SD	Reliability
Working memory span	3.41	2	5	0.79	.66
Belief index	10.79	5	16	3.33	.81
Logic index (neutral)	3.85	1	8	1.84	.57
Logic index (thematic)	7.43	2	14	3.25	.85
Conflict problems	2.23	0	4	1.42	.67
Stop trial accuracy	26.50	19	31	3.33	.63
Primary trial accuracy	55.30	37	64	5.92	
MRT primary trials	649.16	492	801	69.99	
Stop accuracy 250 ms delay	14.16	10	16	1.53	.34
Stop accuracy 150 ms delay	12.33	5	16	2.45	.59
Age (months)	121	110	133	6.44	

measure of stop signal accuracy and accuracy at 150 ms delay were also acceptable. However, the reliability of the accuracy measure at 250 ms delay was below a generally acceptable level. As the descriptive statistics demonstrate, performance at this delay showed a restricted range, with a mean accuracy well above 80%. This undoubtedly explains the lower internal reliability of this measure.

Table 3 shows the pattern of correlations between the working memory span measures, measures of performance on the stop signal task and the age (in months) of the sample. Of particular note, there was no correlation between working memory span and stop signal accuracy at either delay, the key measure of inhibitory control on the task (all $rs < .11$). This suggests that inhibition, as measured by the stop signal task, and working memory capacity, as measured by the counting span, are dissociable constructs and draw on distinct executive processing resources. We will return to this finding in general discussion section that follows.

Although there was no correlation between the main measures of performance on the inhibition and working memory tasks, as Table 3 shows there was a significant negative correlation between working memory span and mean response latency on primary trials on the stop signal task, and a significant positive correlation between working memory and accuracy on these trials. This suggests that children with higher working memory respond more rapidly and with greater accuracy to primary trials.

We turn now to the relationships between the predictor variables and age. Although the age of the sample was restricted in its range (110 to 131 months), significant correlations nevertheless emerged between stop signal accuracy and age. This held for both accuracy at 250 ms and 150 ms delays. It is commonly argued in the literature that inhibitory control develops with age (see, for example, Christ, White, Mandernach & Keys, 2001) and the finding here, particularly given the constrained age range of the sample, is consistent with this assumption. In addition the presence of a significant

TABLE 3
Correlations between working memory, inhibition and age

	1.	2.	3.	4.	5.	6.	7.
1. Working memory span	–						
2. Stop accuracy	.05	–					
3. Accuracy 150 ms delay	.00	.90	–				
4. Accuracy 250 ms delay	.10	.73	.37**	–			
5. Primary trial RT	−.35**	.26*	.20	.24	–		
6. Primary trial accuracy	.26*	.22	.14	.27*	−.30*	–	
7. Age	.14	.42***	.38**	.30*	−.32**	.17	–

$N = 61$, $*p < .05$, $**p < .01$, $***p < .001$.

correlation provides some support for the claim that the stop signal task is tapping into individual differences in inhibitory control.

We turn next to the pattern of correlations between the predictor variables and the indices of performance on the reasoning task. Four indices of performance were derived from the task: a belief index that reflected the number of responses on the thematic problems that coincided with beliefs; a logic thematic index that reflected the number of logical responses given on the problems that had a belief component; a logic neutral index that reflected the number of logical responses on the neutral or arbitrary content problems; and a conflict index that reflected performance on the four reasoning problems in which there was a direct conflict between the logical response and the belief-based response. Recall that we predicted at the outset that working memory would be correlated with reasoning performance, on the assumption that the greater the working memory resource the more able an individual would be to construct an integrated representation of the premises and derive a logical conclusion. As Table 4 shows, the pattern of correlations strongly supports this prediction. Working memory span is highly correlated with logical performance on neutral, thematic, and conflict problems, and negatively correlated with the belief index. This suggests that cognitive capacity is a good predictor of general logical ability and likely a necessary condition for resisting belief based responding.

The pattern of correlations between stop signal accuracy and reasoning are less clear. As Table 4 shows there was no relationship between overall accuracy or accuracy at the 150 ms delay and the reasoning indices. However, accuracy at 250 ms delay was correlated significantly but negatively with the belief index, and positively with the logic thematic index and performance on the conflict problems. There was no relationship between this measure and logical performance on the neutral problems. The pattern of correlations between accuracy at 250 ms delay and the reasoning indices is entirely consistent with the predictions outlined earlier. Those

TABLE 4
Correlations between the reasoning indices and the predictors

	Belief index	Logic thematic	Logic neutral	Conflict problems
Working memory span	−.46***	.44***	.46***	.51***
Stop accuracy	−.21	.12	−.01	.16
Accuracy 150 ms	−.06	−.03	−.09	.03
Accuracy 250 ms	−.36**	.31*	.12	.30*
Age	−.38**	.30*	.19	.24

$N = 61$, *$p < .05$, **$p < .01$, ***$p < .001$.

participants who score highly on the belief index are less accurate and hence less able to inhibit responses to the tone on the stop signal task when it is set at this delay. Those who are more successful at inhibiting give more logical responses on problems in which there is a belief component and conflict problems in which logic and belief suggest alternative responses. In contrast to the correlations with the counting span task, inhibition accuracy at this delay is uncorrelated with logical reasoning on belief-neutral problems. This is exactly as we might expect if we assume that neutral or arbitrary problems do not require the inhibition of information from background knowledge. This is a powerful finding and is even more persuasive if we consider the restriction in range and low reliability of the accuracy measure at this delay (see Table 2).[1] The finding that the pattern of correlations between the inhibition measure and reasoning are mediated by tone delay is in itself an interesting one, and we will return to this in the discussion section that follows.

The next set of analyses we report examined the extent to which stop accuracy and working memory independently predict performance on the reasoning tasks. We performed four multiple regressions with the belief, conflict, logic thematic, and logic neutral indices as the dependent variables and working memory span and accuracy at 250 ms delay as the predictors. Table 5 presents the beta weights for each predictor, the significance level of these weights, the F values, and adjusted R-squared for each model. As Table 4 shows, working memory is a highly significant predictor of each one of these indices. Inhibition accuracy independently predicts a significant proportion of the variance on the belief index, the logic thematic index, and the score on the conflict problems. It is not a significant predictor of logic scores on neutral problems.

The regression confirms the main trends in the correlational analyses, but further demonstrates that working memory and inhibition predict unique aspects of the variance in the reasoning measures derived from the problems with belief-based content. Higher working memory coupled with higher accuracy on the inhibition measure results in less belief-based responding and greater logical accuracy overall, specifically on conflict problems. The findings suggest that working memory capacity is a good predictor of reasoning ability across all problem types, and inhibition specifically predicts performance on problems that require children to resist the influence of their beliefs.

---

[1]The maximum correlation obtainable between two independent measures can be calculated by obtaining the square root of the product of the reliability of these measures. To illustrate, the maximum correlation obtainable between the conflict score and stop signal accuracy at 250ms delay = square root (.67*.34) = .45.

TABLE 5
Summary of the beta weights and *p* values for the counting span and inhibition
measures regressed against the reasoning indices

	Predictors					
	Counting Span		Accuracy at 250ms delay			
Independent variable	Beta weight	p value	Beta weight	p value	F value	R^2 adjusted
Belief index	−.42	<.001	−.31	<.01	$F (2, 58) = 12.72, p<.001$	.28
Logic thematic	.41	<.001	.27	<.02	$F (2, 58) = 10.52, p<.001$	.24
Logic neutral	.46	<.001	.07	>.1	$F (2, 58) = 8.22, p<.001$	.19
Conflict problems	.49	<.001	.26	<.02	$F (2, 58) = 14.25, p<.001$	.31

Whilst these findings are relatively clear, it could be argued that inhibition is not causally related to reasoning performance, but the relationship simply reflects a general developmental increase in the ability to decontextualise thinking. As Table 2 shows, stop signal accuracy is correlated with age and consequently general development might be mediating the relationship between this measure and reasoning. In order to explore this possibility we repeated the regressions, including age as a predictor. Stop signal accuracy remained a significant predictor of the belief index ($\beta = -.24, p < .05$), as did working memory ($\beta = -.40, p < .001$). In this analysis age also emerged as a unique predictor ($\beta = -.26, p < .05$). In the remaining analyses age did not emerge as a significant predictor, but stop signal accuracy remained a marginally significant predictor of performance on the conflict problems ($\beta = .22, p < .06$) and the logic thematic index ($\beta = .22, p < .08$).

In the introduction to this paper we made the claim that the ability to reason irrespective of one's own beliefs and goals is a core cognitive skill that may underlie the development of a range of abilities. In this study our measure of this ability was encapsulated in a simple reasoning task in which both the logical structure and thematic content were manipulated. If we are right in our conjecture that this reasoning measure taps into key educational constructs, then we might expect performance on the task to be correlated with other measures of educational attainment. Table 6 shows the correlations between the reasoning indices and a series of measures of educational attainment amongst a sub-sample of the children who participated in the study ($N = 32$). These measures were available for only one of the schools that took part in the main study and they included a key stage 2 mathematics test, developed by the National Foundation of Educational Research in the UK (NFER), and three teacher-administered

TABLE 6
Correlations between the reasoning measures and measures of educational attainment

	Logic thematic	Logic neutral	Belief index	Conflict problems
NFER maths test	.63***	.54***	−.59***	.39*
Reading	.60***	.28	−.58***	.41*
Writing	.47**	.24	−.48**	.32
Numeracy	.65***	.48**	−.61***	.38*

$N = 32$, *$p < .05$, **$p < .01$, ***$p < .001$.

measures of reading, numeracy, and writing. The scoring for these measures draws on the National Curriculum levels for key stage 2 pupils in primary education in the UK.

The data in Table 6 show a remarkably clear picture. Scores on the belief index show strong negative correlations with the NFER maths test, numeracy, reading, and to a lesser extent writing. A similar pattern emerges with the logic thematic index, and whilst the correlations are weaker, scores on the conflict problems are correlated significantly with three of the four measures. The logic neutral index is significantly correlated exclusively with the maths and numeracy measures. Whilst this analysis is based on a small sample, this may suggest that logical reasoning *per se* is a good predictor of mathematical ability, whilst logical reasoning with belief-based content is a more generic predictor of educational achievement. We will consider the implications of these findings in more detail in the discussion section that follows.

DISCUSSION

The study presented in this paper was undertaken with the aim of examining the relationship between belief-based reasoning and measures of executive function, namely working memory capacity and inhibitory control. The findings present a relatively clear picture. Logical accuracy on reasoning tasks with both arbitrary and belief-based content is highly correlated with working memory capacity, suggesting that the ability to simultaneously hold in mind and manipulate representations is a key factor in the development of reasoning. This finding concurs with recent work that demonstrates that working memory capacity is an important limiting factor in children's reasoning (see, for example, Barrouillet & Lecas, 1999; Barrouillet, Grosset & Lecas, 2000).

The correlational data suggest that working memory predicts reasoning with thematic materials to the same degree as it predicts reasoning with neutral materials. There was little evidence that the ability to decontextualise one's reasoning from beliefs, as measured by a belief index or logical performance on the thematic problems, drew to any greater degree on working memory than reasoning that did not involve decontextualisation. Instead the correlational data suggest that the ability to reason on the basis of the form of the argument, whilst ignoring beliefs, is associated with inhibitory control. Higher accuracy on the stop signal task at the 250 ms delay was associated with a lower score on the belief index and greater logical accuracy on reasoning problems in which belief and logic were in conflict. Importantly stop signal accuracy was uncorrelated with logical performance on neutral problems. The independent contribution of working memory and inhibitory control to successful decontextualisation was confirmed in the regression analysis, where stop signal accuracy at 250 ms delay and counting span emerged as independent predictors for the belief, logic thematic, and conflict indexes. In contrast, logical performance on the belief-neutral problems was predicted uniquely by working memory capacity. These findings suggest that reasoning on belief-based problems draws on two core functions: the ability to inhibit pre-potent or belief-based responses, as reflected in the stop signal task, and the capacity to temporarily store and manipulate representations, as measured by the counting span. This suggests that whilst sufficient cognitive capacity is a necessary prerequisite for accurate performance, it is not sufficient. On thematic problems children must in addition resist the response that the belief system readily cues.

One aspect of the current findings that is somewhat puzzling is that stop signal accuracy at the shorter delay of 150 ms is uncorrelated with reasoning performance, yet accuracy at 250 ms is a good predictor of meaningful aspects of the task. This is despite the fact that the accuracy measure at 250 ms shows a narrower range of scores and is less reliable as a measure of individual differences. Indeed in the context of these characteristics the finding of a correlation between accuracy at this delay and the reasoning indices is particularly powerful. Whilst there may be a number of potential explanations for the different patterns of correlation between the 150 and 250 ms measures, in our view the explanation for these differences lies in the degree to which each measure is a pure reflection of the ability to consciously withhold a response. We would argue that performance on the stop signal task at 250 ms delay is a better measure of this ability than performance at the shorter delay. There are two lines of evidence that form the basis of this claim. The first draws from the literature on the stop signal task, where the average internal response time to the tone has been calculated to be approximately 250 ms (see Nigg, 1999). This corresponds to the longer delay employed in the task used here. Interestingly, differences between accuracy on the stop signal task between groups of typically developing children and children with ADHD, who are commonly thought to suffer from a deficit in inhibition, emerge at delays of 250 ms and above (Aman et al., 1998). This suggests at the very least that length of delay is an important factor, not only in terms of accuracy on the task, but also in terms of providing a measure that distinguishes between groups in which there is both a neurological and functional basis for predicting differences in executive control (see, for example, Tannock, 1998).

A second line of evidence that suggests that the 150 and 250 ms delays may be measuring slightly different aspects of performance arises out of an inspection of the reaction time data for primary trials on the task. In the version of the task used here the stop signal delay was set relative to the mean reaction time in the first block of trials. During the two experimental blocks the delay remained constant. This characteristic of the task led a number of children to delay their response to trials in the experimental blocks to provide a window to enable them to more readily resist responses should a stop signal occur. Overall the difference in primary trial RTs between the first block and the experimental blocks (the slowing effect) was 129 ms. Given that the 250 ms delay falls at a point corresponding to the average internal stop signal response time (Nigg, 1999), on the majority of trials participants will have the opportunity to resist a response irrespective of the degree to which they have strategically slowed their RTs. In contrast, on the 150 ms delay slowing down response latency will have a dramatic effect on the number of trials in which the tone occurs at a point in the RT distribution where conscious withholding of response can be made. What this analysis suggests is that more of the variance on the 150 ms delay will be explained by strategic factors rather than inhibitory control *per se*. Whilst this explanation is tentative, it is nevertheless concordant with the findings discussed above which suggest that delay is an important factor in detecting group differences in inhibitory control (Aman et al., 1998).

In this paper we have argued that the ability to decontextualise thinking from beliefs is associated with inhibitory control. We have also shown that this ability is age-related, even as a function of the narrow age range examined here. Interestingly the literature suggests a remarkable age-related symmetry between accuracy on measures of inhibition and performance on belief-based reasoning tasks. For example, Williams, Ponesse, Schachar, Logan, and Tannock (1999) provided evidence, using the stop signal paradigm, that inhibitory control improves during childhood and declines during late adulthood (see also, Bedard, Nichols, Barbosa, Schachar, Logan & Tannock, 2002). Similarly Christ et al. (2001), while failing to find a difference between children and younger adults, did show a difference in inhibitory control between younger and older adults when processing speed was controlled for in their analysis. Recent research examining age-related changes in belief-based biases in reasoning presents a very similar age-related pattern. Whilst younger children show a much greater propensity to give belief-congruent responses to both informal (Klacynski, Gordon, & Fauth, 1997) and formal reasoning tasks (Moshman & Franks, 1986) than young adults, older adults show a greater number of errors than younger adults specific to problems in which logic and belief dictate different responses (Gilinsky & Judd, 1994; Klacynski & Robinson, 2000).

The evidence of similar developmental patterns in both abilities suggests that the development of inhibitory control is a key factor in contributing to the ability to decontextualise thinking from beliefs. Recent neuro-imaging work provides additional evidence that suggests a neuroanatomical basis both for the role of inhibitory processes in belief-based reasoning and for a functional distinction between reasoning from thematic and neutral materials. Goel and Dolan (2003) examined the functional neuroanatomy of belief-based reasoning using event-related fMRI. Participants were presented with both neutral and belief-laden syllogistic arguments. The key finding was that correct responding on arguments in which logic and belief were in conflict activated an area in the right lateral pre-frontal cortex, a region that has been implicated in tasks that draw on inhibitory functions (Fink et al., 1999). In contrast, correct responses on belief-neutral arguments were uniquely associated with activation in the left superior parietal lobe, an area considered to be involved in the internal representation and manipulation of spatial information.

Goel and Dolan (2003) argued that the distinct patterns of activation associated with different reasoning tasks provide support for accounts of reasoning which posit two distinct processing systems that underlie human reasoning performance. These accounts propose a distinction between two interactive processing systems to explain evidence of both the logical/analytical thinking and the often biased heuristic-based thinking that is characteristic of much of human thought. Under many of these accounts (Evans & Over, 1996; Klacynski & Robinson, 2000; Stanovich, 1999), both systems function to preserve and strengthen existing belief systems, hence belief-consistent information is often processed at a shallow heuristic level, whereas belief-inconsistent information may well activate analytic processing in an attempt to logically disprove a conclusion that cannot be reconciled with an individual's beliefs. Whilst this type of processing may well be common in everyday reasoning it is also the case that many reasoners are able to over-ride the implicit system and respond normatively to problems that require belief-inconsistent responses; that is, some reasoners will engage the analytical system and resist heuristic-based responses. Stanovich (1999; Stanovich & West, 1998) has argued that this ability is strongly related to cognitive capacity or working memory. Those individuals with greater capacity are more likely to resist the heuristic cued response.

The findings of this study suggest something slightly different. Whilst the pattern of correlations clearly shows that working memory capacity predicts logical accuracy on the reasoning tasks, successful reasoning with thematic problems is in addition independently predicted by inhibitory control. This suggests that the ability to inhibit heuristically cued responses is an additional necessary condition for successful reasoning on these problems. Interestingly, as Stonovich has shown amongst adults, thinking disposition also explains unique variance in performance on problems of this kind. In Stanovich's terms, thinking disposition refers to a range of personality characteristics that include openness to ideas, consideration of alternatives, faith in intuition, and cognitive flexibility. An interesting future line of enquiry would be to examine the extent to which inhibitory control, as measured by tasks such as the stop signal task, is itself related to the dispositional characteristics that have been identified as important contributors to belief-independent reasoning.

A final aspect of our data that merits some comment, is the finding that the indices of performance on the belief-based reasoning tasks were highly correlated with indicators of academic success amongst a sub-sample of our population. The measures of educational achievement were based on teacher-administered assessments in mathematics/numeracy, reading, and writing, suggesting that the measure of reasoning that was employed taps into abilities that are related in a very general way to educational success. At the outset of this paper we made the claim that thinking independently of one's beliefs was a core cognitive ability that underpins the development of critical and analytical thinking skills. A reasonable interpretation of the findings here is that the development of executive functions during childhood leads to increased ability to engage in analytical processing, which in turn contributes to increased educational attainment. A potentially fruitful area of development for this work would be to examine the effect of various development psychopathologies on belief-based reasoning tasks of the kind used here. As we have seen, a number of researchers have argued that ADHD, which is often accompanied by low academic achievement, comprises a deficit in behavioural inhibition, and one might expect that such a deficit would lead to highly specific performance detriments in belief-based reasoning. Such work would further clarify the functional role that executive processes play in higher-level cognition.

The executive system remains a relatively poorly defined construct, variously considered responsible for a range of functions associated with the efficient operation of higher-level cognitive processes. There is no doubt that much work remains to be done in identifying both the specific functions associated with the system and the role of these functions in controlling and guiding thought processes. The current work makes a contribution in both of these respects, providing support for the notion of working memory and inhibition as dissociable executive constructs and demonstrating their independent contribution to the successful decontextualisation of thinking.

REFERENCES

Aman, C. J., Roberts, R. J., & Pennington, B. F. (1998). A neuropsychological examination of the underlying deficit in Attention Deficit Hyperactivity Disorder: Frontal lobe versus right parietal lobe theories. *Developmental Psychology, 34*, 956–969.

Baddeley, A. D. (1986). *Working memory*. New York: Oxford University Press.

Barrouillet, P., Grosset, N., Lecas, J. F. (2000). Conditional reasoning by mental models: Chronometric and developmental evidence. *Cognition, 75*, 237–266.

Barrouillet, P., & Lecas, J. F. (1999). Mental models in conditional reasoning and working memory. *Thinking and Reasoning, 4*, 289–302.

Bedard, A., Nichols, S., Barbosa, J. A., Schachar, A., Logan, G. D., & Tannock, R. (2002). The development of selective inhibitory control across the life span. *Developmental Neuropsychology, 21*, 93–111.

Burgess, P. W. (1997). Theory and methodology in executive function research. In P. Rabbitt (Ed.), *Methodology of executive function*. Hove, UK: Psychology Press.

Case , R., Kurland, M., & Goldberg, J. (1982). Operational efficiency and the growth of short-term memory span. *Journal of Experimental Child Psychology, 33*, 386–404.

Christ, S. E., White, D. A., Mandernach, T., & Keys, B. A. (2001). Inhibitory control across the life-span. *Developmental Neuropsychology, 20*, 653–669.

Dias, M. G., & Harris, P.L. (1988). The effect of make-believe play on deductive reasoning. *British Journal of Developmental Psychology, 6*, 207–221.

Dias, M. G., & Harris, P. L. (1990). The influence of the imagination on reasoning by young children. *British Journal of Developmental Psychology, 8*, 305–318.

Evans, J. St. B. T., & Over, D. E. (1996). *Rationality and reasoning*. Hove, UK: Lawrence Erlbaum Associates Inc.

Evans, J. St. B. T., & Perry, T. (1995). Belief bias in children's reasoning. *Cahiers de Psychologie Cognitive, 14*, 103–115.

Fink, G. R., Marshall, J. C., Halligan, P. W., Frith, C. D., Driver, J., Frackowiak, R. S. et al. (1999). The neural consequences of conflict between intention and the senses. *Brain, 122*, 497–512.

Gilinsky, A. S., & Judd, B. B. (1994). Working memory and bias in reasoning across the lifespan. *Psychology and Aging, 9*, 356–371.

Goel, V., Buchel, C., Frith, C., & Dolan, R. J. (2000). Dissociation of mechanisms underlying syllogistic reasoning. *NeuroImage, 12*, 504–514.

Goel, V., & Dolan, R. J. (2003). Explaining modulation of reasoning by belief. *Cognition, 87*(1), B11–B22.

Johnson-Laird, P. N., & Byrne, R. M. J. (1991). *Deduction*. Hove, UK: Lawrence Erlbaum Associates Ltd.

Klacynski, P. A., Gordon, D. H., & Fauth, J. (1997). Goal-oriented reasoning and individual differences in critical reasoning biases. *Journal of Educational Psychology, 89*, 470–485.

Klacynski, P. A., & Robinson, B. (2000). Personal theories, intellectual ability, and epistemological beliefs: Adult age differences in everyday reasoning biases. *Psychology and Aging, 15*, 400–416.

Leevers, H. J., & Harries, P. L. (1999). Persisting effects of instruction on young children's reasoning with incongruent and abstract premises. *Thinking and Reasoning, 5*, 145–173.

Logan, G. D., Cowan, W. B., & Davis, K. A. (1984). On the ability to inhibit simple and choice reaction time responses: A model and a method. *Journal of Experimental Psychology: Human Perception and Performance, 10,* 276–291.

Markovits, H. (2000). A mental model analysis of young children's conditional reasoning with meaningful premises. *Thinking and Reasoning, 6,* 1–14.

Markovits, M., Schleifer, M., & Fortier, L. (1989). Development of elementary deductive reasoning in young children. *Developmental Psychology, 25,* 787–793.

Miyake, A., & Shah, P. (1999). *Models of working memory: Mechanisms of active maintenance and executive control.* Cambridge: Cambridge University Press.

Moshman, D. (1990). The development of metalogical understanding. In W. F. Overton (Ed.), *Reasoning, necessity and logic: Developmental perspectives.* Hillsdale, NJ: Lawrence Erlbaum Associates Inc.

Moshman, D., & Franks, B. A. (1986). Development of the concept of inferential validity. *Child Development, 57,* 153–165.

Nigg, J. T. (1999). The ADHD response-inhibition deficit as measured by the stop task: Replication with DSM-IV combined type, extension and qualification. *Journal of Abnormal Child Psychology, 27,* 393–402.

Pennington, B. F., & Ozonoff, S. (1996). Executive functions and developmental psychopathology. *Journal of Child Psychology and Psychiatry and Allied Disciplines, 37,* 51–87.

Pithers, R. T., & Soden, R. (2000). Critical thinking in education: A review. *Educational Research, 42,* 237–249.

Rabbitt, P. (1997). *Methodology of executive function.* Hove, UK: Psychology Press.

Rust, J., & Golombok, S. (Eds.). (1999). *Modern psychometrics: The science of psychological assessment* (2nd ed.). New York: Routledge.

Stanovich, K. E. (1999). *Who is rational? Studies of individual differences in reasoning.* Mahwah, NJ: Lawrence Erlbaum Associates Inc.

Stanovich, K. E., & West, R. F. (1998). Individual differences in rational thought. *Journal of Experimental Psychology: General, 127,* 161–188.

Tannock, R. (1998). Attention deficit hyperactivity disorder: Advances in cognitive, neurobiological, and genetic research. *Journal of Child Psychology and Psychiatry, 39,* 65–99.

Welsh, M. C., & Pennington, B. F. (1988). Assessing frontal lobe function in children: Views from developmental psychology. *Developmental Neuropsychology, 4,* 199–230.

Williams, B. R., Ponesse, J. S., Schacher, R. J., Logan, G. D., & Tannock, R. (1999). Development of inhibitory control across the life span. *Developmental Psychology, 35,* 205–213.

APPENDIX
The reasoning problems used in the study

Relational problems

Believable True	**Believable False**
Elephants are bigger than dogs	Babies are older than children
Dogs are bigger than mice	Children are older than adults
So, are elephants bigger than mice?	So, are adults older than babies?
Believable indeterminate	**Believable indeterminate**
Cats are bigger than rats	Adults are older than babies
Spiders are bigger than rats	Adults are older than children
So, are cats bigger than spiders?	So, are children older than babies?

Unbelievable True
Houses are bigger than caravans
Caravans are bigger than skyscrapers
So, are houses bigger than skyscrapers?

Unbelievable Indeterminate
Dogs are bigger than mice
Elephants are bigger than mice
So, are dogs bigger than elephants?

Neutral True
Pobs are bigger than Kibs
Kibs are bigger than Wops
So, are Pobs bigger than Wops?

Neutral indeterminate
Zoboles are happier than Risomes
Zapps are happier than Risomes
So, are Zoboles happier than Zapps?

Unbelievable False
Insects are smaller than mice
Mice are smaller than rabbits
So, are rabbits smaller than insects?

Unbelievable indeterminate
Mice are stronger than dogs
Mice are stronger than elephants
So, are dogs stronger than elephants?

Neutral False
Bongos are stronger than Wobbles
Wobbles are stronger than Kabbles
So, are Kabbles stronger than Bongos?

Neutral indeterminate
Pliks are faster than Mibules
Pliks are faster than Ploques
So, are Mibules faster than Ploques?

Conditional problems

Believable True
Cars run on petrol
All things that run on petrol carry people
So, do cars carry people?

Believable Indeterminate
Ducks have beaks
Animals that live near water have beaks
So, do ducks live near water?

Unbelievable True
Teachers read books
People who read books are astronauts
So, are teachers astronauts?

Unbelievable Indeterminate
Birds fly in the sky
Animals that live on the moon fly in the sky
Do birds live on the moon?

Neutral True
Donkeys are hoofed animals
Hoofed animals have fourteen teeth
So, do donkeys have fourteen teeth?

Neutral Indeterminate
Penguins eat a lot
Fat animals eat a lot
So, are penguins fat?

Believable False
Elephants have long noses
Animals with long noses are not heavy
So, are elephants heavy?

Believable Indeterminate
Seat belts are made of nylon
Things that protect us are made of nylon
So, do seat belts protect us?

Unbelievable False
Sparrows are animals
Animals do not live in zoos
So, do sparrows live in zoos?

Unbelievable Indeterminate
Dogs bark
Animals that do not bark have two legs
So, do dogs have two legs?

Neutral False
The Pope lives in Rome
People who live in Rome do not like loud music
So, does the Pope likes loud music?

Neutral Indeterminate
Potatoes are grown in fields
Things that contain chemicals are grown in fields
So, do potatoes contain chemicals?

THINKING & REASONING, 2004, *10* (2), 197–219

Developing reason

Deanna Kuhn, Jared B. Katz, and David Dean Jr.
Teachers College, Columbia University, NY, USA

We argue in favour of the general proposition that the nature of reasoning is best understood within a context of its origins and development. A major dimension of what develops in the years from childhood to adulthood, we propose, is increasing meta-level monitoring and management of cognition. Two domains are examined in presenting support for these claims— multivariable causal reasoning and argumentive reasoning.

Do reasoning skills develop? Putting the question this way, the answer, it seems, must be yes, because the alternatives are implausible. Sophisticated forms of reasoning, such as those required to address the celebrated four-card problem, do not emerge in full flower, nor are they transmitted from external sources in the same manner as factual information. We can debate the exact nature of the process, but few would refute the claim that it is through application and practice that reasoning skills improve. Moreover, the idea that one fully understands mature competencies only by studying their developmental origins has an impressive range of advocates, from traditional constructivists like Werner or Piaget to modern cognitive scientists (Keil, 1998).

It is in this context that we pose here the paradox that the study of adults' reasoning is conducted largely without reference to its development. The consequences range from a restriction in perspective to serious misinterpretation or factual error. One kind of error is practical, as when we assume that a real-life task is within the competence of all adults when in fact the skills necessary to complete it are only incompletely developed in many people. Developmental differences (in rate and endpoint) become the individual variation of adulthood. An example from our own earlier research is juror reasoning (Kuhn, Pennington, & Leadbeater, 1983; Kuhn, Weinstock, & Flaton, 1994).

Correspondence should be addressed to Deanna Kuhn, Teachers College, Columbia University, TC Box 119, New York, NY 10027, USA. Email: dk100@columbia.edu

http://www.tandf.co.uk/journals/pp/13546783.html   DOI: 10.1080/13546780442000015

The other common error is conceptual, when we take for granted as intuitively given forms of reasoning that are in fact hard-won achievements which are years in the making. In this article, we discuss two such cases. One, in which there has been a good deal of empirical research, is multivariable causal reasoning. The other, which has been the subject of very little empirical research to date, is argumentive reasoning.

WHAT DEVELOPS?

Before delving into the specifics of either of these topics, it is well to begin with some preliminaries in the way of a model of development. We propose a general model of the sort depicted in Figure 1 (from Kuhn, 2001). As this model makes clear, more is developing than skills themselves. At a meta-level there is developing understanding of the process (meta-procedural understanding) and product (meta-declarative understanding) that is entailed in the exercise of intellectual skills. Although we do not discuss them here, we claim intellectual values to be a critical part of what develops, as they figure heavily in the disposition, as opposed to the competence, to apply skills (Kuhn, in press).

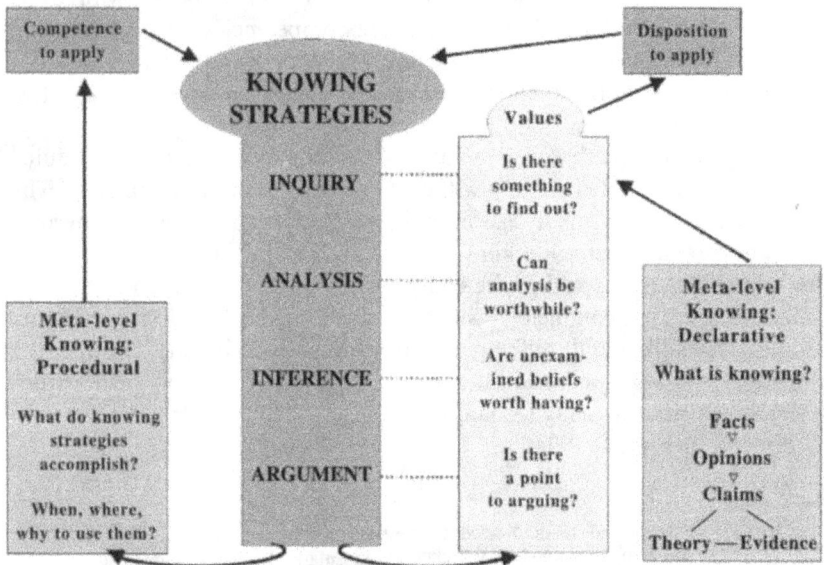

Figure 1. Knowing diagram. From Kuhn, D. (2001). How do people know? *Psychological Science*, *12*(1), 1–8.

Both inductive causal reasoning and argumentive reasoning can be characterised in the most general way as entailing the coordination of theory and evidence (Kuhn, 1989, 2001). Children from an early age construct theories as a means of understanding the world. These theories undergo revision as children interact in the world and encounter evidence bearing on their theories (Gelman & Wellman, 1998). However, in children's early years this process of theory – evidence coordination does not take place at a level of conscious awareness or control. We take gaining metacognitive control over this process to be a major dimension of cognitive development in the years from middle childhood to adolescence (Kuhn, 1989). In terms of the diagram in Figure 1, the meta-level components gradually assume a greater role in monitoring and management of procedural-level skills.

This meta-level of management assumes particular importance in light of the general finding from microgenetic research (Kuhn, Garcia-Mila, Zohar, & Andersen, 1995; Kuhn & Phelps, 1982; Siegler & Crowley, 1991) that individuals have available a range of strategies at any one time that might be brought to bear on a particular problem, implicating a meta-level operator that selects the strategy to be applied on a given occasion. This meta-level operator must also veto other available strategies as incorrect or less effective—a function that figures importantly in the dual-process models of cognitive development proposed by Klaczynski (this issue) and others.

MODELS OF CAUSAL REASONING

In this article we focus on the sample case of multivariable causal reasoning, a topic of great theoretical and practical significance and one that lies at the heart of the general topic of inductive inference. People beginning in early life and continuing throughout their life spans contemplate a wide range of phenomena that intersect in variable ways, and on the basis of this evidence draw conclusions regarding their inter-relations as causes and effects. The task is a dual one of drawing valid inferences and inhibiting invalid ones. How do people do it? This question has been the subject of considerable research and theorising in the adult cognition literature. Although it is reasonable to suppose that these reasoning skills undergo development, it is the mature adult that has been the subject of theoretical models. Moreover, empirical work has relied almost entirely on college populations.

The model that received the most attention is Cheng and Novick's (1990, 1992) "probabilistic contrast" model of multivariable causal inference (MCI), later referred to by Cheng (1997) as the "causal power" theory. According to this theory, within the focal set of events regarded as theoretically relevant by the attributor, inferences of causality are based on estimated differences in the probabilities of the effect in the presence versus the absence of the potential cause. Factors yielding substantial differences across instances will be attributed as causes.

Although Cheng's causal power theory has received the lion's share of attention, several other modern theories of causal inference similarly implicate the constraining influence of theoretical belief and the computation of contrasts between conditions, and are generally consistent with the causal power theory. "Abnormal conditions" (ones absent in a comparison condition), for example, are the basis of the model of causal inference proposed by Hilton and Slugoski (1986). Similarly, models of counterfactual reasoning (Roese & Olson, 1996) rely on comparison of probabilities under two conditions (in which an event does or does not occur), while Bayesian net models (Glymour, 2001; Glymour & Cheng, 1998) also emphasise prior probabilities as constraining computations of causal power.

All of these models share a distinction emphasised by Mackie (1974) and others (Einhorn & Hogarth, 1986) between causes and enabling conditions. In Cheng and Novick's (1992) model, factors that are constant across instances will be either regarded as enabling conditions, if they are perceived as relevant, or dismissed as causally irrelevant (and hence excluded from the focal set). Note that the latter distinction rests entirely on theoretical belief. Covariation within a focal set of instances may provide the basis for a judgement of causality, but when this covariation is absent, theoretical belief offers the only basis for judging whether constant factors are causally relevant (as enabling conditions) or noncausal. This has not been an issue, since inferences of noncausality are in effect treated as non-inferences in such models and accorded little if any attention—a decision we will question here.

The conceptual advance represented by such models is in rejecting covariation alone as sufficient basis for causality and in specifying how knowledge beyond covariation serves to limit the number of covariates inferred to be causal. Theoretical knowledge of a possible causal mechanism appears necessary if a covariate is to be judged causal (Ahn, Kalish, Medin, & Gelman, 1995; Cheng, 1997; Lien & Cheng, 2000). Such knowledge admits a feature to the set considered to be causally relevant and allows the assessment of covariation between feature and outcome to be computed. The problem of causal inference might thus be seen as one of coordinating theoretical understandings of causal mechanism with empirical covariation data (Newsome, 2003; Rehder, 2003).

The goal of Cheng's current work in the MCI paradigm is a far-reaching one: to identify a set of universal inference rules that govern human (and even non-human) causal inference. In Cheng's (1997) words summarising her own effort towards this end, "... the theory I proposed presents a theoretical solution to the problem of causal induction first posed by Hume more than two and a half centuries ago. Moreover, the fact that this theory provides a simple explanation for a diverse set of phenomena regarding human reasoning and Pavlovian conditioning suggests that it *is* the solution adopted biologically by humans and perhaps other animals" (p. 398, italics in original).

Although Cheng's own research based on her model is conducted with college students, there does exist some research following this general paradigm that is an exception to the exclusive use of college students as research subjects. A study by Harris, German, and Mills (1996) and a series of studies by Gopnik and colleagues (Gopnik & Sobel, 2000; Gopnik, Sobel, Schulz, & Glymour, 2001) have examined very young children and highlighted the respects in which their performance appears to conform to Cheng's model and thereby to reveal competent, adult-like causal reasoning.

The data we present here portrays a markedly different picture. Elsewhere (Kuhn & Dean, in press), we have examined in depth the methodological differences that might account for the picture of very early competence presented by Gopnik and Harris and their co-authors, and the picture of incompletely developed skills among older children and even adults presented here. We will not repeat that detailed analysis here, although interested readers may wish to refer to it. In brief summary, the emphasis in the research presented here is on describing and summarising individual patterns of reasoning over time. Research stemming from Cheng's MCI paradigm, in contrast, and consistent with its goal of identifying universal processes, has relied largely on more traditional quantitative methods that confine analysis to closed-ended responses and to the group rather than the individual as the unit of analysis.

Here, we begin by identifying several key attributes that one might expect to characterise a mature mental model of multivariable causality. We then examine data that bear on the extent to which the reasoning of various samples of children and adults conform to the model. Note that we are using the term "mental model" in a more generic manner than is customary (Kuhn, Black, Keselman, & Kaplan, 2000). Typically, the term is invoked to refer to a model of the way in which someone understands some particular phenomenon, such as electricity (Gentner & Gentner, 1983). We have argued that children similarly develop more generic mental models, such as a model of causality, that serve as means for their interpreting a wide range of phenomena and are susceptible to revision, as are more specific mental models.

The following are three key characteristics we propose as attributes of a mature mental model of multivariable causality:

1. Consistency. All else being equal, a cause that produces an effect on one occasion will produce the same effect on another occasion.

2. Additivity. More than one factor may operate on an outcome at a given time or on a given occasion. Normally, the effect of these factors combine, i.e., the total effect is the sum of all individual effects in operation.
3. Interactivity (non-additivity). In some contexts, such as necessary or sufficient or genuinely interactive causes, additivity may not apply and the total effect is not the sum of individual effects.

The mental model of multivariable causality that these attributes reflect, we claim, tends to be taken for granted as in place and operating in all individuals according to models of adult causal cognition such as Cheng's MCI model. We turn now to data that give us reason to question such an assumption.

EXAMINING ASSUMPTIONS OF THE MATURE MENTAL MODEL OF MULTIVARIABLE CAUSALITY

We begin with the third assumption, the distinction between additivity and interactivity, since the relevant data are the most straightforward. Consider college students' responses to the problems in Table 1 (Kuhn, unpublished). The wood-stacking problem (Table 1) is a straightforward one that we also administered to sixth graders and found them readily able to solve by simply adding the individual outputs to determine a joint output when individuals worked together. College students produced this same solution. When the content is transformed to one about chemical pollution, however, the solution becomes indeterminate:

Alt, Bot, & Crel are chemicals that pollute the air and make it dirty.
The first bar shows how much pollution Alt causes.
The second bar shows how much pollution Bot causes.
The 3rd bar shows how much pollution Crel causes.

Two pollutants together may not produce twice the level of pollution as they do individually (there may exist a ceiling on the total amount of pollution), or two together may produce more than twice the level of their individual effects (since in combination they are particularly harmful). However, no sixth graders, and only 3 of 33 college students (09%), recognised this indeterminacy. One college student predicted a particular form of interactive outcome, and the remaining 29 (88%) added the individual effects, producing a solution identical to the one given in the wood-stacking problem. These results are consistent with other findings (Dixon & Tuccillo, 2001; Wilkening, 1981) that even young children are able to predict outcomes based on the joint effects of two variables when they are asked explicitly to do so. Yet the findings

TABLE 1
Wood-stacking problem

Al, Bob, and Chris are stacking wood.
The first bar shows how much Al stacks; the 2nd bar shows how much Bob stacks; the 3rd bar
  shows how much Chris stacks.
Fill in the last 4 bars to show:
How much A&B together stack
How much B&C together stack
How much A&C together stack
How much A, B, & C together stack.

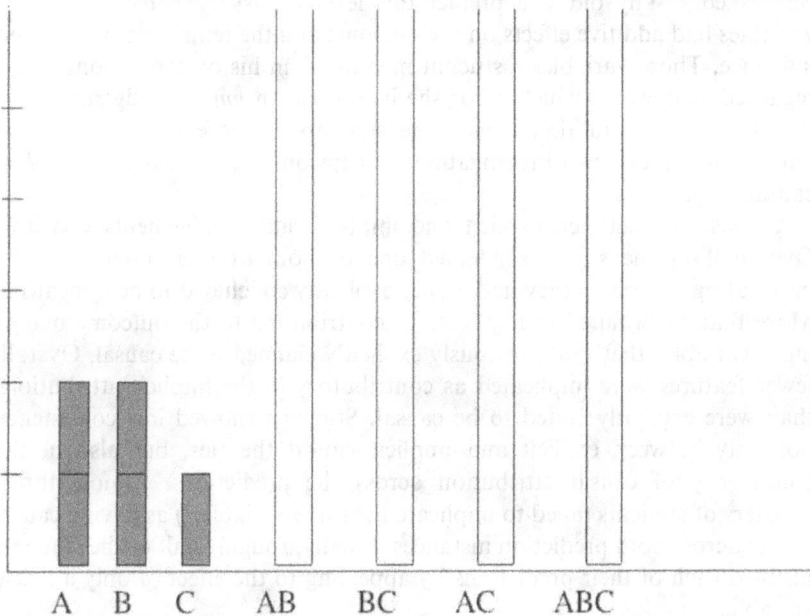

described here indicate that even adults tend not to differentiate additive
and interactive causes when thinking about multiple factors affecting an
outcome.

This lack of differentiation is less surprising when we note that there exist
no natural language equivalents to distinguish the two cases. If we say for
example, "Get a good night's sleep and eat a good breakfast and you'll do
really well," we are neither required nor encouraged to distinguish between
an additive and interactive model as the one we have in mind as applying in
this situation.

At the same time, this example prompts us to ask whether it is really
worth worrying very much about such a distinction—one that even graduate
students in statistics are known to struggle with. Can it make all that much
difference in everyday practical reasoning? As long as the individual causal

agents are taken into account and integrated in some fashion, the result is arguably a good enough approximation to suffice.

We thus turn to the simpler case of multiple variables that act independently on an outcome and are additive in their effects. Keselman (2003) asked sixth graders to investigate and make inferences regarding the causal role of five variables that had been identified within a domain (variables affecting earthquake risk), as well as asking them to make outcome predictions for two new cases representing unique combinations of levels of variables within the domain. After each prediction, the question was asked, "Why did you predict this level of risk?". Three of the five variables had additive effects on the outcome and the remaining two had no influence. Those variables a student mentioned in his or her response were regarded as ones for which he or she had made an *implicit* judgement that the variable was causal. The variables students named earlier as causal (in announcing their post-investigation conclusions) were taken as *explicit* causal judgements.

Consistency between explicit and implicit causal judgements was low. Over half of the students justified one or both of their predictions by implicating a variable they had earlier explicitly concluded to be noncausal. More than 80% failed to implicate as contributing to the outcome one or more variables they had previously explicitly claimed to be causal. Overall, fewer features were implicated as contributory in the implicit attributions than were explicitly stated to be causal. Students showed low consistency not only between explicit and implicit causal theories, but also in the consistency of causal attribution across the predictions. Almost three-quarters of students failed to implicate the same variable(s) as having causal power across both prediction instances. Finally, roughly half of the students justified each of their predictions by appealing to the effect of only a single variable.

If we examine average adults, rather than the typical college students, they do somewhat better (Kuhn & Dean, in press). About half the members of a community choral group, representative of a broad cross-section of the adult population, showed inconsistency in causal attribution in the course of their successive interpretations of accumulating evidence, either at least once initially judging a variable as noncausal and later judging it to be causal, or initially judging a variable as causal and later judging it noncausal, or showing both inconsistencies. Similarly, over half showed inconsistency between implicit and explicit causal judgements. Almost half were inconsistent in causal attributions across three prediction questions. Like the sixth graders, these adults failed to implicate as causal in their implicit attributions as many variables as they needed to in order to yield correct predictions. Over a quarter appealed to the effect of only a single (usually shifting) variable in their prediction judgements, and over half appealed to the effect of only two of the four variables. All of these characteristics of an immature mental model of causality, in contrast, were infrequent in a college student population (Kuhn & Dean, in press).

We can thus point to an inadequate mental model of multivariable causality as a constraint on children's and even many adults' ability to predict effects of multiple variables on an outcome. Additional constraints come into play when individuals are required to bring new evidence to bear on their causal models. The most fundamental is a weakness in metacognitive awareness of new evidence, versus the prevailing mental model, as the basis for one's inferences. And when new evidence is in fact brought to bear on a claim, there emerges the further constraint of faulty inference rules. Notably, factors may be judged causal due simply to their association with the outcome (overattribution) or be judged noncausal because one or more other factors are assumed responsible for the outcome (underattribution, or discounting). In a series of studies (Kuhn, Schauble, & Garcia-Mila, 1992; Kuhn et al., 1995, 2000: Kuhn & Dean, in press), we have asked both children and adults to draw inferences of causality and noncausality when multiple factors are present in conjunction with an outcome, and we have found all of these phenomena to be common.

It is useful to see these weaknesses in a developmental framework. Before saying more about the performance of older participants, we therefore note the results of a study of 4–6-year-olds (Kuhn & Pearsall, 2000). It was hypothesised that children at this young age would fail to distinguish between theoretical explanations and evidence as a basis for their simple knowledge claims, in a parallel way to the confusion between theory and evidence as justifications for causal inferences that we observed in older children and adults. Children were shown a sequence of pictures in which, for example, two runners compete in a race. Certain cues suggest a theoretical explanation as to why one will win, e.g., one has fancy running shoes and the other does not. The final picture in the sequence provides evidence of the outcome, e.g., one of the runners holds a trophy and exhibits a wide grin. When children are asked to indicate the outcome and to justify this knowledge, 4-year-olds show a fragile distinction between the two kinds of justification—"How do you know?" and "Why is it so?"—in other words, the evidence for their claim (the outcome cue in this case) versus their explanation as to why it is plausible (the theory-generating cue). Rather, the two merge into a single representation of what happened, and the child tends to choose as evidence of what happened the cue having greater explanatory value as to why it happened. Thus, in the race example, young children often answered the "How do you know [he won]?" question not with evidence ("He's holding the trophy") but with a theory of why this state of affairs makes sense (e.g., "Because he has fast sneakers").

Similarly, in another set of pictures in which a boy is shown first climbing a tree and then down on the ground holding his knee, the "How do you know [that he fell]?" question was often answered, "Because he wasn't holding on carefully". These confusions between theory and evidence diminish sharply among 6-year-olds, who still make mistakes but the majority of the time distinguish the evidence for their event claim from a theoretical explanation that makes the claim plausible. Findings by other investigators support this characterisation of preschool children as having weak metacognitive control of their own knowing, for example failing to differentiate different sources of their own knowledge claims (Gopnik & Graff, 1988; Whitcombe & Robinson, 2000) and claiming that they had "always known" a piece of information they had just been given (Taylor, Esbensen, & Bennett, 1994).

When older children and adults are asked to coordinate new evidence with their existing mental models of a domain, similar indications are apparent of a fragile meta-level distinction between theory and evidence as the basis for one's inferences. In one of the problems posed to children and adults by Kuhn et al. (1995), for example, participants were asked to identify which of five variables (see Table 2) influenced the popularity of children's TV programmes.

The first programme that Geoff (a pseudonym) selected to examine had commercials but no music or humour, was 2 hours long, and on Tuesday, with a popularity rating of fair. Geoff interpreted this outcome as confirming his earlier expressed theories:

> You see, this shows you that the factors I was saying about, that you have to be funny to make it good or excellent, and the day doesn't really matter, and it's too long.

The second instance Geoff chose added humour and music, and changed the length to a half hour and the day to Wednesday, with an outcome of excellent. Now Geoff concludes, based on the two instances:

> It does make a difference when you put music and have commercials and the length of time and the humour. Basically the day is the only thing that doesn't really matter.

TABLE 2
Causal and noncausal effects in the TV problem (Geoff's problem)

Music (M or −)	Simple causal effect
Commercials (C or −)	Interactive causal effect (causal only in absence of music)
Length (0, 1, 2)	Curvilinear causal effect (0 > 1 = 2)
Day (t or w)	Noncausal
Humour (f or s)	Noncausal

For length variable, $0 = \frac{1}{2}$ hour, $1 = 1$ hour, $2 = 2$ hour. For day variable, t = Tuesday, w = Wednesday. For humour variable, f = funny, s = serious

Geoff thus utilised these two pieces of evidence as an opportunity to confirm all his theories. Three factors that covaried with outcome (music, humour, and length) he interpreted as causal. He also included commercials as causal even though this did not vary, but excluded day of the week, which did vary, as noncausal. He selects data for observation that he believes will "illustrate" the correctness of these theories. To the extent that the outcome data pose interpretive problems, he draws on a variable set of inference rules, applying to each variable those rules that are most protective of his theories. Presence or absence of commercials, for example, is implicated as causal based on its presence in just one successful outcome. When possible, however, in the case of the three other variables also believed causal, Geoff applies the more stringent covariation rule as the basis for inferring causality. As Geoff's reasoning illustrates, the explanatory burden shifts from one variable to another in a way that allows theories to be maintained.

It should be emphasised that in these studies we are not pitting individuals' prior knowledge against new information, asking them to forego the former in favour of the latter. The respondent is free to say, "Here are the implications of your data, but I don't find them convincing, and choose not to modify my theories based on them." Such an individual exhibits the meta-level awareness and management of their own cognition represented in Figure 1. It is the individual who is not aware of how prior beliefs and the presented information relate, because the two have not been represented as distinct entities, who is the cause for concern.

DEVELOPMENTAL COMPARISONS

Our earlier research on causal inferences has been situated in the contexts of scientific reasoning or knowledge acquisition, although we make the case that the forms of reasoning are in many respects identical (Kuhn & Dean, in press). In these studies (Kuhn et al., 1992, 1995, 2000), participants engage in investigation as well as inference, choosing from a database the cases they wish to examine. Although all of the errors that have been described are observed in both children and adults, and the patterns of change observed in microgenetic studies are similar (Kuhn, 1995), overall the performance of adults is superior to that of children.

In a line of current work described here, we have asked whether the same performance patterns can be observed in paper-and-pencil measures. Several different paper-and-pencil instruments have been tried. The most straightforward is the drugs problem in Table 3 and a more difficult one is the reading improvement problem in Table 4, since the former isolates each variable individually and the latter does not.

TABLE 3
Drugs problem

Researchers are trying three new drugs with AIDS patients to see if they improve patients' ability to avoid infections. The names of the drugs are ALON, BENA, and CREL. For a six-month period, some of the patients in the study took all three drugs, some took only two, some took one, and a final group didn't take any. Below are the results for each group. Analyze these results and then answer the questions.

Patients who took ALON, BENA, and CREL:
Average frequency of infections: Low

Patients who took only ALON:
Average frequency of infections: High

Patients who took ALON and BENA:
Average frequency of infections: Medium

Patients who took only BENA:
Average frequency of infections: Medium

Patients who took ALON and CREL:
Average frequency of infections: Medium

Patients who took only CREL:
Average frequency of infections: Medium

Patients who took BENA and CREL:
Average frequency of infections: Low

Patients who took no drug:
Average frequency of infections: High

Did the drug ALON have any effect on patients' ability to avoid infections?
   YES   NO   UNSURE
How do you know?

_____

Did they drug BENA have any effect on patients' ability to avoid infections?
   YES   NO   UNSURE
How do you know?

_____

Did they drug CREL have any effect on patients' ability to avoid infections?
   YES   NO   UNSURE
How do you know?

_____

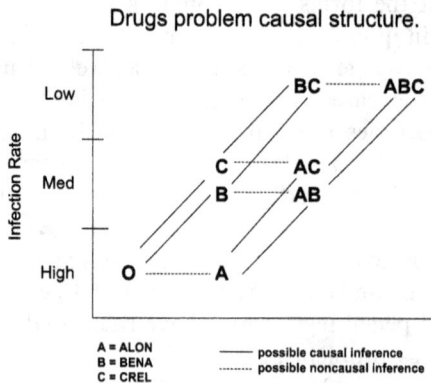

Drugs problem causal structure.

A = ALON
B = BENA
C = CREL

——— possible causal inference
------- possible noncausal inference

TABLE 4
Reading improvement problem

Which factors affect reading performance?

A school district is experimenting with new methods of improving beginning reading instruction. In different classrooms across the district, they are instituting a new reading curriculum, teacher aides, and reduced class size. Here are some preliminary results.

Type	Average reading performance
Regular classrooms	Poor
Classrooms with new curriculum and teacher aid	Greatly Improved
Classrooms with new curriculum and reduced class size	Improved
Classrooms with teacher aide and reduced class size	Improved
Classrooms with new curriculum, teacher aide, and reduced class size	Greatly Improved
Classrooms with teacher aide	Improved

What conclusions do you draw from these findings? Justify your answers by referring to the data.

Is the new curriculum beneficial? How do you know?

Is the teacher aide beneficial? How do you know?

Is the reduced class size beneficial? How do you know?

Reading improvement problem causal structure.

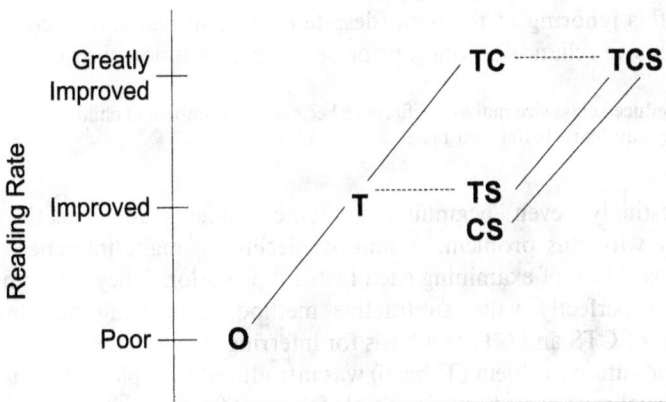

T = Teacher Aide
C = Curriculum
S = Class Size
——— possible causal inference
-------- possible noncausal inference

In the reading improvement problem, community college students very rarely judge class size as having no causal effect (see Table 5). Instead, the overattribution illustrated earlier is the dominant response: Whatever factors are present in the context of an outcome contribute to that outcome. Hence a typical response regarding the new curriculum is:

> Yes it is [beneficial], because all the cases where a new curriculum has been applied the class has improved.

The reasoning is similar with respect to class size, despite its actual noncausal status:

> Class size is also beneficial because according to the data, improvement was evident.

Or,

> Yes, one case shows it [class size] greatly improved performance.

While not displayed at such high levels, underattribution of causality also occurs. The most common basis for it is to ignore the evidence entirely and resort to belief for justification. For example:

> A teacher aide is not beneficial because each teacher has their own method of teaching, so a teacher aide can create confusion.

Even where the data do support exclusion of a factor as having causal power, this ignoring of the data (despite explicit instruction to consider it) and exclusive reliance on one's prior beliefs are common. For example:

> Yes, reduced class size makes a difference because the numbers of children are small so they can learn better and faster.

Interestingly, even beginning graduate students in education have difficulty with this problem. A number decline to make inferences, citing the impossibility of examining each factor in isolation. They were unwilling to use a perfectly valid subtractive method, comparing outcomes for example, of CTS and CT, as a basis for inferring that S had no causal effect.

The pollution problem (Table 6) was introduced to explore the possibility that a visual representation of multiple factors influencing an outcome might facilitate reasoning. As evident in Table 5, at least in this form, it did not. Table 5 summarises performance on the various instruments by a number of different samples (although not all instruments are presented to all groups).

TABLE 5

Performance on causal reasoning problems by problem type and group

Group	N	Evidence-based justification			Valid inclusion			Valid exclusion		
		D	P	R	D	P	R	D	P	R
8th gr	72*	78.9%	58.3%		18.3%	2.8%		11.3%	0.0%	
CC	60*	82.1%		61.7%	46.2%		8.3%	7.7%		3.3%
Grad	216	94.0%	88.1%	93.1%	48.8%	28.6%	27.3%	20.2%	22.6%	10.6%
AD	84									

Group	N	Invalid inclusion (theory-based)			Invalid inclusion (evidence-based)			Invalid exclusion (theory-based)		
		D	P	R	D	P	R	D	P	R
8th gr	72*	5.6%	9.7%		29.6%	60.6%		19.7%	23.6%	
CC	60*	5.1%		31.7%	38.5%		56.7%	7.7%		8.3%
Grad	216	0.0%	0.0%	4.6%	25.0%	32.1%	52.3%	3.6%	6.0%	11.1%
AD	84									

D = Drugs problem, P = Pollution problem, R = Reading problem *Drugs N: 8th = 71, CC = 39. Percentages are based on total number of responses. CC = urban community college students. Grad = beginning graduate students in education. AD = community adults (members of a choral group).

TABLE 6 (below and opposite)
Pollution problem

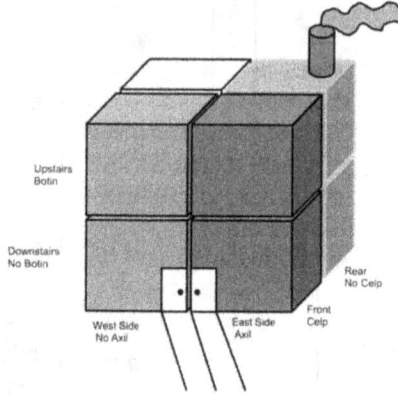

Upstairs
Botin

Downstairs
No Botin

Rear
No Celp

Front
Celp

West Side
No Axil

East Side
Axil

A factory uses three different chemicals to make its product, gumball machines. In the different parts of the factory, different chemicals are needed for the work done in that section of the factory.

In all of the sections on the east side of the factory, Axil is used.

In all of the sections in the upstairs floor of the factory, Botin is used.

In all of the sections in the front of the factory, Celp is used. (See picture)

So, for example, someone who worked downstairs on the east side front section of the factory would be exposed to Axil and to Celp, but not to Botin.

The factory owners are worried about air pollution in the factory. As you can see from the picture, the pollution is worse (darker colour) in some sections of the factory and not as bad in other sections (lighter colours).

Based on what you see, answer the following questions.

Does the chemical **Axil** have any effect on the amount of pollution in the factory?
YES   NO   UNSURE
How do you know?

_____

_____

Does the chemical **Botin** have any effect on the amount of pollution in the factory?
YES   NO   UNSURE
How do you know?

_____

_____

Does the chemical **Celp** have any effect on the amount of pollution in the factory?
YES   NO   UNSURE
How do you know?

_____

_____

_____

Pollution problem causal structure

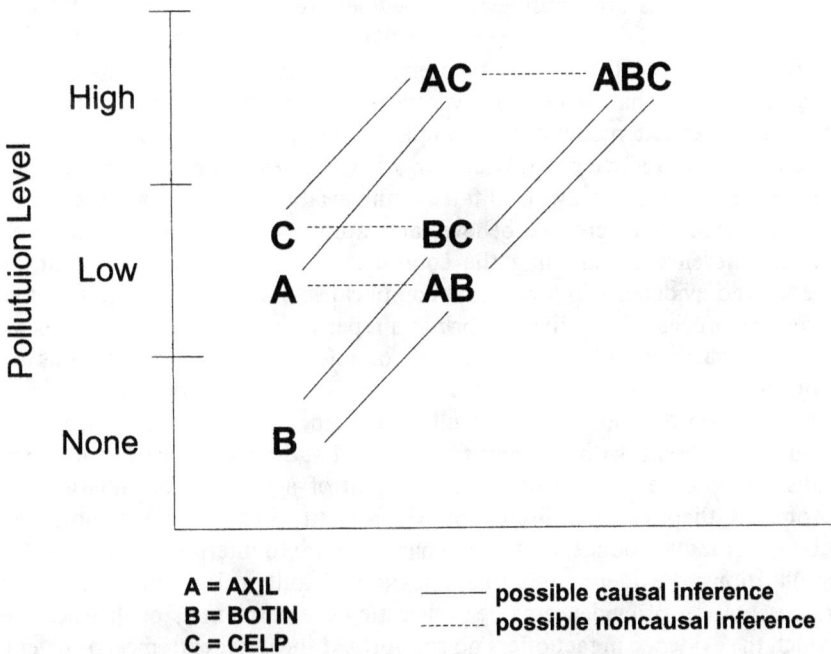

A = AXIL
B = BOTIN
C = CELP

———— possible causal inference
- - - - - possible noncausal inference

These data are consistent with the pattern suggested earlier. Developmental differences appear, although even adults continue to make errors.

IMPLICATIONS FOR UNDERSTANDING CAUSAL INFERENCE

The implicit assumption underlying research in the adult causal inference literature is that people's understanding of multiple causality reflects a standard scientific model: Multiple effects may contribute to an outcome in an additive manner—as long as background conditions remain constant, these effects are expected to be consistent, i.e., the same antecedent does not affect an outcome on one occasion and fail to do so on another, or affect the same outcome differently on one occasion than another. (A more complex model, encompassing interaction effects, presumes understanding of the simpler main effects of an additive model.) Indeed, all of science is predicated on such a model. It is not clear how the world would operate in the absence of these assumptions, and hence it is not surprising that research on human causal inference has implicitly adopted such a model as a starting point. Nonetheless, the findings described here suggest that it is a mistake to do so.

Recognition of the role of theoretical understanding of mechanism in causal inference has been seen by causality researchers such as Cheng as providing needed reduction in complexity of a general model of causal inference. By reducing the number of variables considered as causal candidates, theory may facilitate multivariable causal inference. The findings described here, we believe, are more consistent with a model of causal inference as entailing the coordination of the two components—theory and evidence—in a way that complicates, more than it simplifies, the inference process. An individual brings a repertoire of inference strategies or rules (of varying validity) to the task of interpreting the implications of evidence, and these may be drawn on selectively in the service of theory – evidence coordination. As a result, consistency in causal attribution is commonly absent, with different rules applied at different times for different causal candidates, as expedient in the goal of achieving coordination by protecting theories from discrepant evidence. At its extremes, the coordination effort may produce, on the one hand, failure to interpret accurately the implications of evidence, due to application of faulty rules, with consequent representation of evidence as demonstrating the correctness of theories for which the evidence in fact offers no support. At the other extreme, consistent interpretation of evidence is achieved through exclusive application of valid inference rules and implications for theory are recognised. In the former case, theory and evidence are not clearly distinguished. In the latter, they are perfectly coordinated (even if the individual decides theory modifications may not be warranted by the evidence). The majority of cases, however, are likely to be intermediate between these two extremes, reflected in intra-individual variability in inference rules used, but with some accurate interpretation of the implications of evidence.

Consistent with such a model is a more subtle and variable role of theoretical belief than the one postulated by Cheng's MCI model. Theory – evidence coordination is a complex, dynamic process, with the role of theory not confined to an initial phase in which variables are excluded from consideration on theoretical grounds. Our data reveal frequent instances of an individual's shift from an earlier declaration of a variable as noncausal to a subsequent claim that it is causal. Thus, variables that are initially excluded are not necessarily forgotten. Evidence may continue to be evaluated with respect to their causal status. Conversely, the frequently observed shift from an early declaration of a variable as causal to a subsequent judgement of noncausality indicates that judgements of noncausality are not in fact exclusively theory-based (Kuhn & Dean, in press; Kuhn et al., 1995).

Although intra-individual variability is common in intellectual functioning (Siegler, 1994) and need not require specific explanation, at least some
intra-individual variability, we have proposed, is attributable to individuals' imperfect skills in coordinating theories and evidence. Confinement
to a university population, as is typical in the adult cognition literature,
may reduce—although it does not eliminate—this variability. The
distribution of usage of strategies or rules of differing effectiveness within
an individual may change over time, as it is seen to do in microgenetic
studies (Kuhn, 1995; Kuhn et al, 1995; Siegler & Crowley, 1991). It is here
especially that we see the value of a developmental framework, which
allows both intra-individual and inter-individual variation among adults to
be interpreted developmentally. In this light, we have as much to learn
from adults as we do from children with respect to how reasoning skills
develop. It is this perspective that has led us to devote so much attention
to the thinking of adults in an article in which we are arguing for the value
of a developmental perspective.

PARALLELS IN THE DEVELOPMENT OF
ARGUMENTIVE REASONING

Space does not permit us to examine argumentive reasoning in as great
detail as we have causal reasoning. A very brief review is nonetheless
worthwhile to illustrate that the case we have made for a developmental
framework is not limited to the topic of inductive causal inference. Although
much less empirical research has been done on argument, the parallels are
instructive.

Like causal inference, argument is widely accepted as a basic form of
human reasoning that does not need to be learned. The term "argument"
of course is used to refer to two quite different acts. An individual
constructs an argument to support a claim. The dialogic process in which
two or more people engage in debate of opposing claims can be referred
to as argumentation or argumentive discourse to distinguish it from
argument as product. Nonetheless, implicit in argument as product is the
advancement of a claim in a framework of evidence and counterclaims
that is characteristic of argumentive discourse, and the two kinds of
argument are intricately related (Billig, 1987; Kuhn, 1991). Most
empirical research on argument has been devoted to argument as
product.

Paralleling the case of causal inference, rudimentary skills of argument, of
both process and product types, have been widely taken for granted as
within the competence of children as well as adults. Empirical research with
children has focused on demonstrating the competence of very young
children to appropriately justify their claims and even to engage in effective

argumentation (Eisenberg & Garvey, 1981; Orsolini, 1993; Stein & Miller, 1993).

Research examining the arguments (as products) of adolescents and adults, in contrast, report serious weaknesses. In supporting a claim, respondents commonly fail to construct two-sided arguments or to distinguish evidence and explanation in support of their claims (Brem & Rips, 2000; Kuhn, 1991, 2001; Kuhn, Shaw, & Felton, 1997; Perkins, 1985; Voss & Means, 1991). They also show wide susceptibility to belief bias (Klaczynski, 2000). Relatively little research, however, has been devoted to the more complex skills that are involved when one undertakes to guide the process of competitively co-constructing an argument in the context of discourse.

According to Walton (1989), skilled argumentation has two goals. One is to secure commitments from the opponent that can be used to support one's own argument. The other is to undermine the opponent's position by identifying and challenging weaknesses in his or her argument. Drawing on Walton's analysis, Felton and Kuhn (2001) and Kuhn and Udell (2003) identify two potential forms of development in argumentive discourse skills. One is enhanced understanding of discourse goals and the other is application of effective strategies to meet these goals. These two forms of development can be predicted to reinforce one another. Progress in use of discourse strategies is propelled by a better understanding of discourse goals. At the same time, exercise of these strategies in discourse promotes more refined understanding of the goals of argumentive discourse.

To examine development in argumentive discourse skills, Felton and Kuhn (2001) conducted a cross-sectional comparison of the dialogues of young teens and community college young adults arguing about capital punishment. The results revealed striking differences between the two groups. Teens' discourse focused largely on the arguments supporting their own position, at the expense of addressing the arguments of their opponents. Teens appear to interpret the goal of argumentive discourse as prevailing over an opponent by superior presentation of one's own position. This objective, if successfully met, undermines the opponent's position, but without addressing the opponent's argument.

Adults, in contrast, in addition to advancing their own arguments, were more likely to address the opponent's argument, most often through counterargument. In undertaking to undermine their opponent's argument, as well as advance their own argument, adults' dialogues thus came closer to achieving the dual goals of argumentive discourse. These appear to be skills that need to develop during childhood and adolescent years. Deep-level processing of the opponent's argument, in addition to articulating one's own argument and negotiating the mechanics of discourse, may represent cognitive overload for the novice arguer.

Based on these findings, Kuhn and Udell (2003) undertook an experimental study with young adolescents. Following a several-month-long intervention designed to exercise and develop their argumentation skills, participants showed a decrease in the proportion of dialogue devoted to exposition, that is, articulation and clarification of one's own position and perspective. Furthermore, they showed an increase in the proportion of dialogue devoted to challenges that address the partner's claims and seek to identify weaknesses in them, reflecting understanding of Walton's (1989) second goal of argumentation.

This research has helped us to understand the cognitive skills involved in dialogic argumentation. In the present context, their significance lies in the case we have undertaken to make for a developmental perspective in the study of informal (or formal, for that matter) reasoning. The perspective is simply captured. To fully understand a mature competency, watch it develop.

REFERENCES

Ahn, W-k., Kalish, C. W., Medin, D. L., & Gelman, S. A. (1995). The role of covariation versus mechanism information in causal attribution. *Cognition, 54*, 299–352.

Billig, M. (1987). *Arguing and thinking: A rhetorical approach to social psychology.* Cambridge: Cambridge University Press.

Brem, S. K., & Rips, L. J. (2000). Explanation and evidence in informal argument. *Cognitive Science, 24*(4), 573–604.

Cheng, P. W. (1997). From covariation to causation: A causal power theory. *Psychological Review, 104*(2), 367–405.

Cheng, P. W., & Novick, L. R. (1990). A probabilistic contrast model of causal induction. *Journal of Personality and Social Psychology, 58*, 545–547.

Cheng, P. W., & Novick, L. R. (1992). Covariation in natural causal induction. *Psychological Review, 99*, 365–382.

Dixon, J., & Tuccillo, F. (2001). Generating initial models for reasoning. *Journal of Experimental Child Psychology, 78*, 178–212.

Einhorn, H. J., & Hogarth, R. M. (1986). Judging probable cause. *Psychological Bulletin, 99*, 3–19.

Eisenberg, A. R., & Garvey, C. (1981). Children's use of verbal strategies in resolving conflicts. *Discourse Processes, 4*, 149–170.

Felton, M., & Kuhn, D. (2001). The development of argumentive discourse skill. *Discourse Processes, 32*(2&3), 135–153.

Gelman, S. A., & Wellman, H. M. (1998). Enabling constraints for cognitive development and learning: Domain specificity and epigenesis. In D. Kuhn & R. S. Siegler (Eds.), *Handbook of child psychology: Cognition, language, and perception* (5th ed., Vol. 2). New York: Wiley.

Gentner, D., & Gentner, D. R. (1983). Flowing waters or teeming crowds: Mental models of electricity. In D. Gentner & A. L. Stevens (Eds.), *Mental models.* Hillsdale, NJ: Lawrence Erlbaum Associates Inc.

Glymour, C. (1998). Learning causes: Psychological explanations of causal explanation. *Minds and Machines, 8*, 39–60.

Glymour, C. (2001). *The mind's arrows: Bayes nets and graphical causal models in psychology.* Boston, MA: MIT Press.

Glymour, C., & Cheng, P. W. (1998). Causal mechanism and probability: A normative approach. In M. Oaksford & N. Chater (Eds.), *Rational models of cognition* (pp. 296–313). Oxford: Oxford University Press.

Gopnik, A., & Graf, P. (1988). Knowing how you know: Young children's ability to identify and remember the sources of their beliefs. *Child Development, 59*(5), 1366–1371.

Gopnik, A., & Sobel, D. M. (2000). Detecting blickets: How young children use information about novel causal powers in categorization and induction. *Child Development, 71*(5), 1205–1222.

Gopnik, A., Sobel, D. M., Schulz, L. E., & Glymour, C. (2001). Causal learning mechanisms in very young children: Two-, three-, and four-year-olds infer causal relations from patterns of variation and covariation. *Developmental Psychology, 37*(5), 620–629.

Harris, P. L., German, T., & Mills, P. (1996). Children's use of counterfactual thinking in causal reasoning. *Cognition, 61*, 233–259.

Hilton, D. J., & Slugoski, B. R. (1986). Knowledge-based causal attribution: The abnormal conditions focus model. *Psychological Review, 93*(1), 75–88.

Keil, F. C. (1998). Cognitive science and the origins of thought and knowledge. In R. M. Lerner (Ed.), *Handbook of child psychology: Theoretical models of human development* (5th ed., Vol. 1). New York: Wiley.

Keselman, A. (2003). Supporting inquiry learning by promoting normative understanding of multivariable causality. *Journal of Research in Science Teaching, 40*(9).

Klaczynski, P. A. (2000). Motivated scientific reasoning biases, epistemological beliefs, and theory polarization: A two-process approach to adolescent cognition. *Child Development, 71*(5), 1347–1366.

Kuhn, D. (1989). Children and adults as intuitive scientists. *Psychological Review, 96*, 674–689.

Kuhn, D. (1991). *The skills of argument.* Cambridge: Cambridge University Press.

Kuhn, D. (1995). Microgenetic study of change: What has it told us? *Psychological Science, 6*, 133–139.

Kuhn, D. (2001). How do people know? *Psychological Science, 12*(1), 1–8.

Kuhn, D. (in press). *Education for thinking.* Cambridge, MA: Harvard University Press.

Kuhn, D., Black, J., Keselman, A., & Kaplan, D. (2000). The development of cognitive skills to support inquiry learning. *Cognition and Instruction, 18*(4), 495–523.

Kuhn, D., & Dean, D. (in press). Connecting scientific reasoning and causal inference research. *Journal of Cognition and Development.*

Kuhn, D., Garcia-Mila, M., Zohar, A., & Andersen, C. (1995). Strategies of knowledge acquisition. In *Monographs of the Society for Research in Child Development* (Vol. 60).

Kuhn, D., & Pearsall, S. (2000). Developmental origins of scientific thinking. *Journal of Cognition and Development, 1*, 113–129.

Kuhn, D., Pennington, N., & Leadbeater, B. (1983). Adult thinking in developmental perspective: The sample case of juror reasoning. In P. Baltes & O. Brim (Eds.), *Life-span development and behavior* (Vol. 5). New York: Academic Press.

Kuhn, D., & Phelps, E. (1982). The development of problem-solving strategies. *Advances in Child Development and Behavior, 17*, 1–44.

Kuhn, D., Schauble, L., & García-Mila, M. (1992). Cross-domain development of scientific reasoning. *Cognition and Instruction, 9*(4), 285–327.

Kuhn, D., Shaw, V., & Felton, M. (1997). Effects of dyadic interaction on argumentive reasoning. *Cognition and Instruction, 15*, 287–315.

Kuhn, D., & Udell, W. (2003). The development of argument skills. *Child Development, 74*(5), 1245–1260.

Kuhn, D., Weinstock, M., & Flaton, R. (1994). How well do jurors reason? Competence dimensions of individual variation in a juror reasoning task. *Psychological Science, 5*, 289–296.

Lien, Y., & Cheng, P. W. (2000). Distinguishing genuine from spurious causes: A coherence hypothesis. *Cognitive Psychology, 40*(2), 87–137.

Mackie, J. L. (1974). *The cement of the universe: A study of causation.* London: Oxford University Press.

Newsome, G. L. (2003). The debate between current versions of covariation and mechanism approaches to causal inference. *Philosophical Psychology, 16*(1), 87–107.

Orsolini, M. (1993). "Dwarfs don't shoot": An analysis of children's justifications. *Cognition and Instruction, 11*(3&4), 281–297.

Perkins, D. N. (1985). Post-primary education has little impact upon formal reasoning. *Journal of Educational Psychology, 77*, 563–571.

Rehder, B. (2003). Categorization as causal reasoning. *Cognitive Science, 27*, 709–748.

Roese, N. J., & Olson, J.M. (1996). Counterfactuals, causal attributions, and the hindsight bias: A conceptual integration. *Journal of Experimental Social Psychology, 32*, 197–227.

Siegler, R. S. (1994). Cognitive variability: A key to understanding cognitive development. *Current Directions in Psychological Science, 3*(1), 1–5.

Siegler, R. S., & Crowley, K. (1991). The microgenetic method: A direct means for studying cognitive development. *American Psychologist, 46*(6), 606–620.

Stein, N. L., & Miller, C. A. (1993). The development of memory and reasoning skill in argumentative contexts: Evaluating, explaining, and generating evidence. In R. Glaser (Ed.), *Advances in instructional psychology.* Hillsdale, NJ: Lawrence Erlbaum Associates Inc.

Taylor, M., Esbensen, B. M., & Bennett, R. T. (1994). Children's understanding of knowledge acquisition: The tendency for children to report that they have always known what they have just learned. *Child Development, 65*(6), 1581–1604.

Voss, J., & Means, M. (1991). Learning to reason via instruction in argumentation. *Learning and Instruction, 1*, 337–350.

Walton, D. N. (1989). Dialogue theory for critical thinking. *Argumentation, 3*, 169–184.

Whitcombe, E. L., & Robinson, E. J. (2000). Children's decisions about what to believe and their ability to report the source of their belief. *Cognitive Development, 15*(3), 329–346.

Wilkening, F. (1981). Integrating velocity, time, and distance information: A developmental study. *Cognitive Psychology, 13*(2), 231–247.

THINKING & REASONING, 2004, *10* (2), 221–239

From inference to reasoning:
The construction of rationality

David Moshman
University of Nebraska, Lincoln, USA

Inference is elementary and ubiquitous: Cognition always goes beyond the data. Thinking—including problem solving, decision making, judgement, planning, and argumentation—is here defined as the deliberate application and coordination of one's inferences to serve one's purposes. Reasoning, in turn, is epistemologically self-constrained thinking in which the application and coordination of inferences is guided by a metacognitive commitment to what are deemed to be justifiable inferential norms. The construction of rationality, in this view, involves increasing consciousness and control of logical and other inferences. This metacognitive conception of rationality begins with logic rather than ending with it, and allows for developmental progress without positing a state of maturity.

For Piaget, cognitive development was, at its core, the development of logicality, culminating in the formal operational logic that emerges in early adolescence (Inhelder & Piaget, 1958). Piaget's theory of formal operations has been challenged by the results from two major bodies of literature. One, the early competence literature, purports to show that, contrary to Piaget, even preschool children are fundamentally logical. The other, the adult irrationality literature, purports to show that, contrary to Piaget, even adults are at best nonlogical, if not fundamentally illogical and thus irrational. If these literatures challenge Piaget's conception of formal operations, however, they seem to pose an equally serious challenge to each other. If preschool children are so logical, how could adults be so illogical?

The short answer, I think, is that logical *inference* is routine even among preschool children, but that logical *reasoning*, as I will define it in this article, continues to develop for many more years and remains imperfect even in adults. More generally, we will see how preschool logic and adult

Correspondence should be addressed to David Moshman, Department of Educational Psychology, 230 Teachers College Hall, University of Nebraska, Lincoln, NE 68588, USA. Email: dmoshman1@unl.edu

© 2004 Psychology Press Ltd
http://www.tandf.co.uk/journals/pp/13546783.html   DOI: 10.1080/13546780442000024

nonlogicality are consistent with each other and with developmental conceptions of progress in rationality.

LOGIC AND RATIONALITY

Is rationality nothing more than logic? According to Bickhard and Campbell (1996, pp. 400–401):

> [W]hatever the merits of a 'mental logic' account of specific kinds of thinking at specific points in human development, it can't be telling the whole story about human reasoning. When broader historical and developmental trends are taken into account, it becomes clear why rationality cannot be simply assimilated to logicality. A system of formal logic already contains all of its valid theorems. Logical systems don't grow or become more powerful. Logical systems can't construct new logical systems more powerful than themselves. Yet the history of logic shows that human knowledge of logic and logical systems has developed (Bochenski 1970, Kneale and Kneale 1986) and that more and more powerful systems of logic have been discovered. If rationality simply means following the rules contained within a particular logical system, then the history of logic can't be rational!
>
> Similarly, if being rational means being logical, the development of each individual's knowledge of logic can't be a rational process either ...

Consistent with this view of rationality as something more than logic, developmental research indicates that a conception of rationality as logical inference would greatly overestimate the rationality of young children and greatly underestimate the extent of ongoing development in reasoning. In a series of two experiments, for example, Pillow (2002) presented a total of 112 children, ranging in age from 5 through 10 years, with a series of inference tasks, including a deduction task in which they saw two toys of different colours, which were then hidden in two cans. After looking into one of the cans they were asked about the colour of the toy in the other can. Every child, regardless of age, inferred the colour correctly.

This result was no surprise to Pillow, whose concern was the development of metalogical understanding *about* deductive inferences (see below). In fact there is substantial evidence that preschool children routinely make deductive inferences (Braine & O'Brien, 1998; Hawkins, Pea, Glick, & Scribner, 1984; Scholnick & Wing, 1995) and that even the behaviour patterns of infants show an increasingly coordinated sensorimotor logic (Langer, 1980, 1986).

But even if there is a sense in which the behaviour of an infant is in accord with strict rules of logic, the infant is not aware of that logic. Similarly, when preschool children reach correct conclusions, they don't even know they have made an inference, much less know anything about the nature, purpose, or justifiability of that inference. As we will see below, what develops beyond early childhood is not the basic ability to make logical inferences, but metalogical knowledge about the nature and justifiability of logical inferences, and metacognitive awareness, knowledge, and control of one's inferential processes.

If by rationality we mean conformity to rules of logic, then even preschool children are substantially rational in their inferential processes. If by rationality we mean metacognitive awareness, knowledge, and control of inferential processes, however, then rationality develops over a period of many years that often extends well beyond childhood without ever attaining a definitive state of maturity (Kuhn, 2000; Moshman, 1994). Such a conception does not deny an important role for logic but goes beyond logic in two ways. First, even within the logical domain, a metacognitive conception of rationality locates rationality in metalogical understanding and control rather than in logic *per se*. Second, a metacognitive conception acknowledges that rationality may develop through reflection on and coordination of heuristics and norms more subtle than the rules of formal logic. As we will see, this conception helps us understand how progress towards rationality is consistent with both logical competence in young children and inferential diversity among adults.

INFERENCE, THINKING, AND REASONING

Inference—going beyond the data—is elementary and ubiquitous. By the end of their first year, if not long before, infants infer what they will see from what they hear, and vice versa, infer the locations of objects from partial information, and infer people's emotions from their facial expressions. The uses of inference continue and expand with age. In reading and conversation we make inferences about meaning. In planning we make inferences about the future. In remembering we make inferences about the past. Cognition, in all its forms, is inferential.

Thinking is the deliberate application and coordination of one's inferences to serve one's purposes (Moshman, 1995, in press-a). We see this in problem solving, decision making, judgement, planning, argumentation, and other self-consciously inferential activities. What all of these have in common is metacognition, broadly construed to encompass "the achievement of increasing awareness, understanding, and control of one's own cognitive functions, as well as awareness and understanding of these functions as they occur in others" (Kuhn, 2000, p. 320). With the development of metacognition over the course of childhood and beyond, there is progress in the quality of our thinking, although this is not a matter of approaching some mature state of perfect thinking (Klaczynski, in press).

Reasoning is epistemically self-constrained thinking (Moshman, 1995, in press-a). When thinkers constrain their inferences with the intent of conforming to what they deem to be appropriate inferential norms, they can be said to be reasoning. Reasoning, then, requires *epistemic cognition*—knowledge about the fundamental nature and justifiability of knowledge and inference.

Epistemic cognition has been the topic of substantial research and theory in developmental and educational psychology for the past several decades (Chandler, Hallett, & Sokol, 2002; Hofer & Pintrich, 1997, 2002; King & Kitchener, 1994; Kuhn, Cheney, & Weinstock, 2000). Epistemic development, it turns out, begins early and has a long history. Even preschool children, at least by age 4, understand that people lacking information may have, and act on the basis of, false beliefs (Flavell, Miller, & Miller, 2002; Mitchell & Riggs, 2000). Over the course of childhood, recognising the inferential nature of their own cognitive processes, they construct a constructivist theory of mind. By late childhood, children understand that they are active constructors of knowledge (Chandler et al., 2002; Kuhn, 2000).

Although preadolescents are aware of, and have explanations for, differing interpretations in particular cases, they do not theorise about the nature, limits, and justification of knowledge in the abstract. Adolescents and adults, however, construct explicit epistemologies (Chandler et al., 2002; Hofer & Pintrich, 1997, 2002; King & Kitchener, 1994; Kuhn et al., 2000). The first to appear, and one common among adolescents and adults of all ages, is an objectivist epistemology, in which ultimate truth is deemed to be directly observable, provable, and/or known to the authorities. Differences of opinion can only be the result of mistakes. Recognising the intrinsic subjectivity of knowledge, however, some people construct subjectivist epistemologies, in which truth, which is constructed from individual and/or cultural perspectives, is deemed to be determined by, and thus relative to, such perspectives. Finally, recognising the nihilistic and self-refuting nature of radical subjectivism, some people construct rationalist epistemologies that, without any claim to absolute or final truth, posit that ideas and viewpoints can be meaningfully evaluated, criticised, and justified.

Any epistemology provides a basis for reasoning—for deliberately constraining one's inferential processes in the name of truth. Rationalist epistemologies presumably support better reasoning than objectivist or subjectivist epistemologies, but there are many rationalist epistemologies, many forms of advanced reasoning, and many bases for error and misjudgement. Thus development proceeds from inference to thinking to reasoning, but these are not stages in any simple sense. Thinking and reasoning develop throughout childhood and often well beyond, and there is always room for greater consciousness of how one is making one's inferences and why.

THE DEVELOPMENT OF METALOGICAL UNDERSTANDING

As we have seen, there are a wide variety of justifiable inferences, providing a basis for broad conceptions of thinking, reasoning, and rationality that go far beyond the realm of logic. It seems clear, however, that logical inferences are, in some circumstances, among those that can be most convincingly justified, and that knowledge about the nature and use of such inferences is thus an important basis for reasoning. In this section we narrow our focus to consider an important aspect of epistemic development—the development of metalogical understanding (Moshman, 1990).

Metalogical understanding—conceptual knowledge about logic—includes (1) awareness of inference as a process that generates conclusions from premises; (2) understanding that some inferences are better than others; (3) knowledge about the logical properties of propositions, inferences, and arguments; and (4) conceptualisations of logic as an epistemic domain. Let us consider each of these in turn, beginning with awareness of inference and of the associated distinction between premises and conclusions.

People of all ages routinely construct structures of knowledge that include, but go beyond, available facts. This is a long-standing truism of cognitive psychology (Jenkins, 1974), and there is no doubt that it holds for children (Beal, 1990; Flavell et al., 2002). In reading a text, for example, readers make inferences as they read, such that textual information and associated inferences are intertwined, often inextricably, in the resulting mental representation. Having read that Alphaville is north of Boomtown, and that Boomtown is north of Metropolis, a reader may construct a mental representation of Alphaville north of Boomtown north of Metropolis and read off that Alphaville is north of Metropolis. From an external perspective we may observe that "Alphaville is north of Metropolis" is a conclusion inferred from "Alphaville is north of Boomtown" and "Boomtown is north of Metropolis". From the perspective of the reader, however, these are simply three facts that can be read off the mental representation constructed in the course of processing the text. There is often no need to distinguish conclusions from premises, and no awareness of the inferential processes that have generated the former from the latter.

Even when adults are unaware of their inferences, however, they are aware that they make inferences. Even when they fail to distinguish their conclusions from their premises, they understand, in principle, the distinction between these. Preschool children, in contrast, are not just unaware of particular inferences but seem unaware of inference itself. They don't simply lose track of what they have inferred from what; they fail to make a distinction between premises and conclusions. The difference is not that very young children are unable to make inferences or even that they are less likely than adults to do so. The difference is that very young children are unaware of inferential processes, both their own and those of others, and thus fail to distinguish the output of such processes from the input.

By age 6, however, children recognise inference as a potential source of knowledge for both themselves and others (Keenan, Ruffman, & Olson, 1994; Miller, Hardin, & Montgomery, 2003; Pillow, 1999, 2002; Pillow, Hill, Boyce, & Stein, 2000; Sodian & Wimmer, 1987). Sodian and Wimmer (1987) devised a simple but revealing methodology for assessing young children's awareness of inference. Imagine that you are presented with a container of red balls. A ball is then removed from this container and placed in an opaque bag without your seeing which ball was transferred. Despite the absence of perceptual input, you readily infer that the ball in the bag is red. Moreover, because you are aware that this conclusion can be inferred, you recognise that another person who also did not see the transfer will make the same inference you did and will know the colour of the ball in the bag without having seen it.

Sodian and Wimmer presented variations on this task, including a variety of control tasks, to children aged 4 to 6 years. They found that children of 4 or 5 years routinely made correct inferences about the colour of the ball in the bag but showed no recognition that another person could infer that colour. Even when the other person correctly indicated the colour of the ball, they attributed this to a lucky guess. In contrast, 6-year-olds not only made the correct inference but recognised that the other person would make the same inference and thus, despite not having seen the ball in the bag, would know its colour. In a variation of the task involving nonidentical objects in the original container, moreover, 6-year-olds recognised that the other person would not be able to infer the colour of the transferred object. Even though they themselves had seen and thus knew the colour of the transferred object, they understood that the other person would not have that knowledge.

Even the 4-year-olds in Sodian and Wimmer's study, however, understood that perception could be a source of knowledge—that a person who had seen the transferred ball would know its colour even if they themselves did not. This result is consistent with extensive research on early theories of mind showing that preschool children, beginning at age 4, understand that what a person knows is a function of what the person has seen, and that people with different perceptual access may thus have different beliefs, including false beliefs (Mitchell & Riggs, 2002). Although it has been suggested that children as young as age 4 also have some awareness of inference as a source of knowledge (Keenan et al., 1994), the evidence for this is open to serious question (Pillow, 1999). Most subsequent research has confirmed that awareness of inference begins to be seen at age 6, and there is evidence that even 6-year-olds are sometimes oblivious to inferences recognised by older children. Awareness of inference apparently emerges about age 6, later than what is commonly called "theory of mind", and continues to develop through the childhood years (Beal, 1990; Miller et al., 2003; Pillow, 1999, 2002; Pillow et al., 2000).

Awareness of inference allows one to consider the possibility that some inferences are better than others, in the epistemic sense that the conclusions they generate are more justifiable. In a series of two experiments, Pillow (2002) presented sets of inference-related tasks to 112 children, ranging in age from 5 to 10 years, and to 16 college undergraduates. The tasks included deductive inference, inductive inference, guessing on the basis of partial information, and pure guessing. Children of all ages, as well as adults, were highly certain of their conclusions in the case of deductive inferences and less certain in the case of nondeductive inferences and guesses. Even the youngest children (ages 5–6) had significantly more confidence in deductions than in guesses and justified their deductive conclusions by referring to relevant premises. By ages 8–10, children had significantly more confidence in deduction than induction and significantly more confidence in induction than in pure guessing. Adults showed a clear hierarchy with certainty significantly higher for deductive than for inductive inferences, for inductive inferences than for informed guesses, and for informed guesses than for pure guesses. Related research is consistent with the conclusion that children have at least some intuition of the greater certainty associated with deduction as early as age 5 or 6, but that understanding of various metalogical distinctions—deduction versus induction, inference versus guessing, informed versus pure guessing—continues to develop across childhood and beyond (Galotti, Komatsu, & Voeltz, 1997; Pillow et al., 2000).

Deductive inferences are not just better than nondeductive inferences in the sense of allowing a somewhat higher level of certainty, however. In the case of a deductive inference, the conclusion follows necessarily from the premises. Motivated initially by the centrality of necessity in Piaget's (1987, 2001) theory (Smith, 1993), there has been substantial research on the development of conceptions of necessity. Miller, Custer, and Nassau (2000), for example, interviewed 100 children of ages 7, 9, and 11 about logical necessities (e.g., a light must be on or not on), mathematical necessities (e.g., 3 is bigger than 2), definitional necessities (e.g., triangles have three sides), physical laws (e.g., letting a pencil go will result in it falling), social conventions (e.g., students wear shoes in school), and an arbitrary fact (whether there was chalk in a particular box). Questions focused on spatial universality ("Is this true everywhere?"), changeability ("Could this ever change?"), and the imaginability of any alternative (including, for a sample of items, a request to draw an alternative such as "a triangle that does not have three sides"). Even the 7-year-olds showed some appreciation of necessary truths as holding everywhere and never changing. With increasing age, children made increasingly sophisticated differentiations among the various sorts of knowledge and increasingly recognised that violations of necessary truths were literally unimaginable.

Other research has generated results consistent with this picture. Children show some understanding of logical necessity, consistency, and impossibility beginning about age 6 (Ruffman, 1999; Somerville, Hadkinson, & Greenberg, 1979; Tunmer, Nesdale, & Pratt, 1983). Research also shows continuing development in the comprehension of necessity, possibility, sufficiency, indeterminacy, and associated concepts over the remaining years of childhood (Byrnes & Beilin, 1991; Morris & Sloutsky, 2001; Piaget, 1987; Pieraut-Le Bonniec, 1980; Ricco, 1997; Ricco, McCollum, & Wang, 1997), and age-related constraints on the ability to learn such concepts (Klahr & Chen, 2003).

Not surprisingly, the development of metalogical understanding continues into adolescence. Consider the following arguments, each consisting of two premises and a conclusion:

1. Elephants are plants or animals.

   Elephants are not plants.

   Therefore, elephants are animals.

2. Elephants are animals or plants.

   Elephants are not animals.

   Therefore, elephants are plants.

Even a young child would readily endorse the first argument as logical. Children as old as age 9 or 10, however, reject arguments such as #2 as illogical (Moshman & Franks, 1986). Most adolescents and adults, on the other hand, especially given sufficient opportunity to consider their responses, recognise in cases of this sort that the two arguments have the same logical form and are both valid. The second argument has a false second premise and a false conclusion, which is why children reject it, but it is nonetheless a valid argument in that the conclusion follows necessarily from the two premises. If the premises were true, the conclusion would necessarily be true as well.

This age difference does not reflect an inability of children with regard to particular logical forms. Very young children routinely make instantaneous deductions without even realising they have done so. But that's precisely the problem. Lacking awareness of inference, they cannot explicitly evaluate arguments. Even as children gain some degree of awareness of and control over their inferences, they initially remain oblivious to the logical form of those inferences. They make disjunctive inferences, for example, without explicit awareness of the logical form of disjunctive arguments. Lacking explicit awareness of logical form, children do not distinguish form from content and thus remain centred on immediate inferences from empirically acceptable propositions (see Harris & Leevers, 2000, for research on counterfactual inference in young children, and Simoneau & Markovits, 2003, for research on the complexities of subsequent development).

As children approach adolescence they increasingly distinguish form from content, and thus can recognise valid arguments even in the case of arguments containing false premises and/or a false conclusion (Morris, 2000). At relatively advanced levels of metalogical understanding, typically beginning about age 11, it becomes possible to recognise and evaluate the logical interconnections among propositions that are hypothetical or even false (Efklides, Demetriou, & Metallidou, 1994; Franks, 1996, 1997; Markovits & Bouffard-Bouchard, 1992; Markovits & Nantel, 1989; Markovits & Vachon, 1989; Moshman & Franks, 1986). As a result, adolescents and adults are able to consider the potential interrelations of multiple possibilities and thus to formulate and test explicit theories (Inhelder & Piaget, 1958; Kuhn, Amsel, & O'Loughlin, 1988; Moshman, 1998, in press-a; Zimmerman, 2000).

Even in early childhood, then, automatic inferences are routine. In middle childhood there is awareness of, and increasing knowledge about, inference. Adolescents and adults, notwithstanding their many shortcomings, routinely show systematic forms of hypothetico-deductive reasoning not seen in children under the age of about 11. Is there still another stage, attained at least by some logicians, involving perhaps an explicit conception of logic as an epistemic domain, a mode of justification? Whether or not there is such a stage, or *any* highest stage, each stage in the sequence represents an advance in consciousness and control of logic, and thus a higher level of rationality than the stage from which it emerged.

UNIVERSALITY AND DIVERSITY

Piaget famously posited a universal sequence of stages culminating in a universal state of maturity—formal operations (Inhelder & Piaget, 1958). In a universalist stage model such as Piaget's, each stage can only emerge from the previous one, and the limitations of each stage, if they are ever to be understood, can only be understood from the perspective of the next, so development proceeds in a predictable sequence, with the highest stage defining the state of maturity. Individuals may differ in the rate and extent of development, but development, to the extent that it occurs, can only proceed along a single path.

Research on the development of metalogical understanding suggests a picture consistent with a universalist stage model. Preschool children make inferences but are not aware of doing so. Beginning at about age 6, children become aware of inference, increasingly understand that some inferences are better than others, increasingly recognise the necessity of deductive inferences, and increasingly comprehend associated forms of necessity, possibility, and impossibility. Beginning at about age 11, at least some individuals attain a more explicit understanding of the role of logical form in guaranteeing the validity of deductive arguments and show increasingly systematic reasoning with hypothetical and false premises. The three stages run parallel, in important ways, to Piaget's preoperational, concrete operations, and formal operations stages, and it seems plausible that they form an invariant sequence. That is, children make inferences before they come to understand the logical properties of inferences, and they understand those properties before they apply such metalogical understanding in hypothetical contexts. Moshman (1990) provides a metacognitive account of such a sequence, including a fourth stage that reflects on the third from the standpoint of a logician.

As we have seen, however, logical inferences are not the only legitimate inferences. Rationality includes metacognitive knowledge and control of a variety of inferences. Rationality is thus much richer than logic, and its development can be expected to be more diverse.

Many theorists have suggested that human inferential processes are usefully construed as comprising two fundamental systems (Evans, 2002; Kahneman, 2003; Klaczynski, 2000, 2001, in press; Sloman, 1996; Stanovich, 1999; Stanovich & West, 2000). Although the distinction between the systems can be, and has been, formulated in a variety of ways, one system is generally seen as analytical, involving the strict application of logic and other mechanistic systems of formal rules, and the other as heuristic, involving processes that are associative, holistic, flexible, and sensitive to context. The distinction between two inferential systems raises questions about the locus of diversity. One possibility is that some groups of people are oriented towards analytic processing and other groups towards heuristic processing. Another possibility is that individuals differ in this regard but that such differences exist mostly within, rather than across, abstract social groups. A third possibility is that inferential diversity exists mostly within, rather than across, individuals. Diversity, in other words, may exist primarily across groups, across individuals, or within individuals.

Theorists of group differences fall into two categories—those highlighting culture and those highlighting gender. Cultural difference theorists construe current evidence as showing categorical distinctions in inference, thinking, and reasoning across discrete cultural groups (Nisbett, Peng, Choi, & Norenzayan, 2001; Peng & Nisbett, 1999). Nisbett et al. (2001, p. 291, italics in original), for example,

... find East Asians to be *holistic*, attending to the entire field and assigning causality to it, making relatively little use of categories and formal logic, and relying on "dialectical" reasoning, whereas Westerners are more *analytic*, paying attention primarily to the object and the categories to which it belongs and using rules, including formal logic, to understand its behavior. The 2 types of cognitive processes are embedded in different naive metaphysical systems and tacit epistemologies.

Interestingly, this distinction parallels one commonly made by some feminist theorists with regard to what they see as a categorical distinction between male and female reasoning. Construing logic as masculine, gender difference theorists have argued that the equation of rationality with logic is central to the oppression of women because men, who tend to be logical, are thereby deemed rational, whereas women, who tend towards inferential processes that are more holistic, flexible, and contextual, are thereby deemed less rational (Oliver, 1991; Orr, 1995). Given the existence of males and females in all cultures, it is unclear how the positions of the cultural difference theorists and the gender difference theorists can be reconciled. For the most part these two subcategories of group difference theorists appear unaware of each other and do not address each other's views.

Claims of categorical group differences in inferential processes can turn out to be false if research shows there is really only one mode of processing—for example, if seemingly heuristic inferences always turn out to be logical after all. However, even when the inferential diversity is real—as it seems in this case to be—there are two ways in which claims of categorical group differences can turn out to be wrong. With regard to the standard analytic vs heuristic dichotomy, one possibility is that there are indeed some people who can be deemed analytical/formal thinkers and others who can be deemed heuristic/contextual thinkers, but that both types of people are commonly found in the various groups alleged to be categorically different. Another possibility is that both modes of processing are common in most or all people. In this case, although we can still distinguish two types of thinking, a distinction between two types of thinkers is more misleading than helpful.

Research supports the latter possibility. Both analytic/formal and heuristic/contextual processes are commonly seen in most or all people (Evans, 2002; Klaczynski, 2000, 2001, in press; Stanovich, 1999; Stanovich & West, 2000). There are indeed individual differences in the use of these processes, and some of these differences may be related to culture and/or gender, but neither East Asians, Westerners, women, nor men have been shown to rely on any particular kind of reasoning to the exclusion of any other kind. On the contrary, studies of thinking and reasoning routinely fail to find gender differences (Klaczynski, 2001), and even where cultural differences are found (Nisbett et al., 2001; Peng & Nisbett, 1999) they are virtually never categorical. Both analytic and heuristic processes are routine in most or all women and most or all men in most or all cultural contexts.

Inferential diversity, moreover, may be too rich to capture in a simple distinction between analytic and heuristic processes, or any other dichotomy. Moshman (1998) distinguished three forms of reasoning— *case-based, law-based*, and *dialectical*. This can be transformed into four by dividing case-based reasoning into (a) *analogical reasoning*, in which previous cases serve heuristic purposes, as in solving a problem by considering the solution to a similar one, and (b) *precedent-based reasoning*, in which earlier determinations constrain the legitimacy of later ones, as in the resolution of legal disputes in a system of case law. We can generate five categories of reasoning if we also subdivide law-based reasoning into (a) *ruled-based reasoning*, in which thinking is constrained by formal rules such as those of logic and mathematics, and (b) *principled reasoning*, in which thinking is constrained by abstract principles such as those associated with advanced moral understanding (Moshman, in press-b). Dialectical reasoning, in turn, takes multiple forms that can be sorted into any number of additional categories. Many researchers and theorists, moreover, see thinking as an ongoing interchange of multiple strategies which vary over time (Kuhn, Garcia-Mila, Zohar, & Andersen, 1995; Siegler, 1996).

How many domains of inference or types of thinking or forms of reasoning are there? No matter how we put the question, there is no right answer. The impossibility of a right answer should not deter us from trying to develop taxonomies and theories of thinking and reasoning, but we should be wary of assumptions that there are precisely two kinds of thinking, or any other particular number.

In sum, research on thinking and reasoning demonstrates diversity within individuals, diversity of a sufficiently subtle sort that it cannot be reduced to some small number of definitive categories. This picture has important implications for understanding (a) human universality, (b) the process of thinking, and (c) the process of development.

Classic notions of universality, based on a universal logic that defines rationality, do not deny the possibility of erroneous inferential processes but are challenged by the existence of legitimate inferential diversity. It does not appear that Piaget's conception of formal operations, or any other logical structure, constitutes rational maturity. Interestingly, however, the fact that we all use diverse strategies and perspectives renders human diversity a human universal. Inferential diversity, it turns out, is a universal characteristic of human rationality.

Attention to internal diversity—the diversity within each of us—is important to understanding processes of thinking and development. Thinking, it appears, is not the deliberate application of the one true logic but rather involves the coordination of distinct inferential processes. Given the demands of such coordination, it is to be expected that we would each, perhaps to varying degrees, develop metacognitive understanding and control of our diverse inferences.

The development of rationality, then, is not a matter of switching over from one sort of inferential system to another, as in a transition from heuristic to analytic processing. Rather it is a matter of increasing consciousness and control of multiple inferential processes, as in the coordination of heuristic and analytic processing. We are now prepared to consider developmental processes more directly.

THE CONSTRUCTION OF RATIONALITY

How do we come to be rational? As we have seen, far from being its culmination, logic comes early in the development of rationality. By the age of 4, if not earlier, children routinely make logically correct verbal inferences. Increasingly sophisticated forms of logic can be identified, in fact, in the sensorimotor coordinations of infancy (Langer, 1980, 1986; Piaget, 1936/1963).

The transition from inference to reasoning, as we have seen, is not a transition from illogical inference to logical inference or from heuristic inference to analytic inference. Rather it is the development of increasingly explicit knowledge of properties implicit in the variety of inferences we already make. Novelty resides not in facts or skills that emerge from genes or are taken in from environments, but rather in emerging conceptual knowledge about inferential abilities we already had. It seems likely, then, that progress in reasoning and rationality comes about through reflection on our inferences. Such reflection, for example, might enable an individual to determine that a particular inference is logically necessary because there is only one possible conclusion, and further reflection may enable the formulation of a more general coordination of necessity and possibility (Piaget, 1987).

If the only legitimate inferences were those sanctioned by a particular logical system, ideal reasoning might consist simply of assimilating premises to that system. As we have seen, however, thinking and reasoning involve the coordination of diverse inferences. Reflection on reasoning, then, must include reflection on such coordinations, and may generate knowledge that facilitates and improves future coordinations. Thus the development of rationality is as much a process of coordination as a process of reflection, and these cannot be sharply distinguished (Piaget, 1985, 2001).

Reflection and coordination, moreover, often take place in the context of social interaction, and especially peer interaction. In social contexts we may find ourselves challenged to justify our conclusions, and thus to recognise and justify our inferences. We may also be challenged to understand the inferential paths that led others to alternative views, and to coordinate those inferences and conclusions with ours. Thus social interaction may substantially encourage processes of reflection and coordination.

Not all social interactions promote rationality, however. If the interacting individuals differ in knowledge, authority, or power (as in child/adult, student/teacher, and novice/expert interactions), the lower-status individual may simply accept the conclusions of the higher-status individual with little or no reflection on or coordination of inferential processes. Thus the kind of social interaction most likely to promote the construction of rationality may be peer interaction—ideally, interaction among individuals who are, and see themselves to be, comparable in knowledge, authority, and power.

Processes of reflection and coordination in the context of peer interaction are illustrated in a study by Moshman and Geil (1998) in which college students were presented with the original and most difficult version of the notorious selection task, which requires logical testing of an abstract hypothesis. Consistent with previous research, only 3 of the 32 students who worked individually correctly determined what evidence to seek. In sharp contrast, 15 out of the 20 groups of five or six students each who worked collaboratively made correct selections, even in cases where no member of a group initially gave the logical response, and individual members of these groups generally understood why their final selections were correct. Close examination of what happened within the groups showed a process of collaborative reasoning in which students presented, justified, criticised, compared, and combined a variety of ideas and possibilities until they achieved a structure of logical understanding that most or all members of the group understood and accepted.

In sum, the construction of rationality involves ongoing processes of reflection, coordination, and peer interaction (Moshman 1998, in press-a; Piaget, 1985, 2001). These generate progress towards higher levels of metacognitive understanding and control of our inferential processes, but they do not culminate in any final logical structure. Whatever level of rationality we attain, further reflection on and coordination of our current skills and insights can enhance our (meta)rationality.

This is a constructivist view of the development of rationality in that it relies not on genetic or environmental forces but on self-regulated processes of reflection and coordination. Like Piaget's theory and other developmental versions of constructivism, the present view highlights the rationality of the constructive processes and their success in generating progress towards higher levels of rationality. Unlike Piaget's theory, however, the present view does not assume a universal sequence of general stages or a universal structure that constitutes maturity. Thus the present approach represents what I have elsewhere called pluralist rational constructivism (Moshman, in press-a).

THE UBIQUITY OF INFERENCE

Developmental theories are theories of progress and thus highlight the ways we get better—more logical, more rational, or something of that sort. For a full view of human functioning, however, it is important to keep in mind that not everything changes, and that not all changes are good. Even as our abilities to think and reason improve with age, we continue throughout our lives to be driven by inferences beyond our present knowledge and control. Genetic considerations may be important in some cases, as in the universal human capacity for inferring emotions from the sight of human facial expressions. Cultural considerations, such as being indoctrinated in the ways and/or beliefs of a religious, political, or other group, may also drive systems of automatic inference and block ideologically unacceptable inferences. Even as we construct beliefs and values of our own, self-serving biases direct our inferences to avoid conflict with our identities (Klaczynski, 1997, 2000; Klaczynski & Narasimham, 1998; Moshman, 2004).

With development we become conscious of some of our inferences and better control our beliefs and self-conceptions. Progress is always possible through reflection, coordination, and peer interaction, but we can never fully conceptualize and control our inferences. Even as we become conscious of the basis for some set of inferences, that consciousness itself generates new inferences of which we are not (yet) conscious.

Thinking and reasoning always arise in the context of diverse systems of inference that are deeply biological, cultural, and self-serving. Even as we progress towards greater rationality, thinking and reasoning remain just the tip of an inferential iceberg. Logic is elementary, and further development achievable, but rational maturity forever eludes us.

REFERENCES

Beal, C. R. (1990). Development of knowledge about the role of inference in text comprehension. *Child Development, 61*, 1011–1023.

Bickhard, M. H., & Campbell, R. L. (1996). Developmental aspects of expertise: Rationality and generalization. *Journal of Experimental and Theoretical Artificial Intelligence, 8*, 399–417.

Bochenski, I. M. (1970). *A history of formal logic*. New York: Chelsea.

Braine, M. D. S., & O'Brien, D. P. (Eds.). (1998). *Mental logic*. Mahwah, NJ: Lawrence Erlbaum Associates Inc.

Byrnes, J. P., & Beilin, H. (1991). The cognitive basis of uncertainty. *Human Development, 34*, 189–203.

Chandler, M. J., Hallett, D., & Sokol, B. W. (2002). Competing claims about competing knowledge claims. In B. K. Hofer & P. R. Pintrich (Eds.), *Personal epistemology: The psychology of beliefs about knowledge and knowing* (pp. 145–168). Mahwah, NJ: Lawrence Erlbaum Associates Inc.

Efklides, A., Demetriou, A., & Metallidou, Y. (1994). The structure and development of propositional reasoning ability: Cognitive and metacognitive aspects. In A. Demetriou & A. Efklides (Eds.), *Intelligence, mind, and reasoning: Structure and development* (pp. 151–172). Amsterdam: North-Holland.

Evans, J. St. B. T. (2002). Logic and human reasoning: An assessment of the deduction paradigm. *Psychological Bulletin, 128*, 978–996.

Flavell, J. H., Miller, P. H., & Miller, S. A. (2002). *Cognitive development* (4th ed.). Upper Saddle River, NJ: Prentice Hall.

Franks, B. A. (1996). Deductive reasoning in narrative contexts: Developmental trends and reading skill effects. *Genetic, Social, and General Psychology Monographs, 122*, 75–105.

Franks, B. A. (1997). Deductive reasoning with prose passages: Effects of age, inference form, prior knowledge, and reading skill. *International Journal of Behavioral Development, 21*, 501–535.

Galotti, K. M., Komatsu, L. K., & Voelz, S. (1997). Children's differential performance on deductive and inductive syllogisms. *Developmental Psychology, 33*, 70–78.

Harris, P. L., & Leevers, H. J. (2000). Reasoning from false premises. In P. Mitchell & K. J. Riggs (Eds.), *Children's reasoning and the mind* (pp. 67–86). Hove, UK: Psychology Press.

Hawkins, J., Pea, R. D., Glick, J., & Scribner, S. (1984). "Merds that laugh don't like mushrooms": Evidence for deductive reasoning by preschoolers. *Developmental Psychology, 20*, 584–594.

Hofer, B. K., & Pintrich, P. R. (1997). The development of epistemological theories: Beliefs about knowledge and knowing and their relation to learning. *Review of Educational Research, 67*, 88–140.

Hofer, B. K., & Pintrich, P. R. (Eds.). (2002). *Personal epistemology: The psychology of beliefs about knowledge and knowing.* Mahwah, NJ: Lawrence Erlbaum Associates Inc.

Inhelder, B., & Piaget, J. (1958). *The growth of logical thinking from childhood to adolescence.* New York: Basic Books.

Jenkins, J. J. (1974). Remember that old theory of memory? Well, forget it! *American Psychologist, 29*, 785–795.

Kahneman, D. (2003). A perspective on judgment and choice: Mapping bounded rationality. *American Psychologist, 58*, 697–720.

Keenan, T., Ruffman, T., & Olson, D. R. (1994). When do children begin to understand logical inference as a source of knowledge? *Cognitive Development, 9*, 331–353.

King, P. M., & Kitchener, K. S. (1994). *Developing reflective judgment: Understanding and promoting intellectual growth and critical thinking in adolescents and adults.* San Francisco: Jossey-Bass.

Klaczynski, P. A. (1997). Bias in adolescents' everyday reasoning and its relationship with intellectual ability, personal theories, and self-serving motivation. *Developmental Psychology, 33*, 273–283.

Klaczynski, P. A. (2000). Motivated scientific reasoning biases, epistemological beliefs, and theory polarization: A two-process approach to adolescent cognition. *Child Development, 71*, 1347–1366.

Klaczynski, P. A. (2001). Analytic and heuristic processing influences on adolescent reasoning and decision-making. *Child Development, 72*, 844–861.

Klaczynski, P. A. (in press). Metacognitive and cognitive variability: A two-process model of decision making and its development. In J. E. Jacobs & P. A. Klaczynski (Eds.), *The development of decision making.* Mahwah, NJ: Lawrence Erlbaum Associates Inc.

Klaczynski, P. A., & Narasimham, G. (1998). Development of scientific reasoning biases: Cognitive versus ego-protective explanations. *Developmental Psychology, 34*, 175–187.

Klahr, D., & Chen, Z. (2003). Overcoming the positive-capture strategy in young children: Learning about indeterminacy. *Child Development, 74*, 1275–1296.

Kneale, W., & Kneale, M. (1986). *The development of logic*. Oxford: Clarendon.

Kuhn, D. (2000). Theory of mind, metacognition, and reasoning: A life-span perspective. In P. Mitchell & K. J. Riggs (Eds.), *Children's reasoning and the mind* (pp. 301–326). Hove, UK: Psychology Press.

Kuhn, D. Amsel, E., & O'Loughlin, M. (1988). *The development of scientific thinking skills*. San Diego, CA: Academic Press.

Kuhn, D., Cheney, R., & Weinstock, M. (2000). The development of epistemological understanding. *Cognitive Development, 15*, 309–328.

Kuhn, D., Garcia-Mila, M., Zohar, A., & Andersen, C. (1995). Strategies of knowledge acquisition. *Monographs of the Society for Research in Child Development, 60*, Serial No. 245.

Langer, J. (1980). *The origins of logic: From six to twelve months*. San Francisco: Academic Press.

Langer, J. (1986). *The origins of logic: One to two years*. Orlando, FL: Academic Press.

Markovits, H., & Bouffard-Bouchard, T. (1992). The belief-bias effect in reasoning: The development and activation of competence. *British Journal of Developmental Psychology, 10*, 269–284.

Markovits, H., & Nantel, G. (1989). The belief-bias effect in the production and evaluation of logical conclusions. *Memory & Cognition, 17*, 11–17.

Markovits, H., & Vachon, R. (1989). Reasoning with contrary-to-fact propositions. *Journal of Experimental Child Psychology, 47*, 398–412.

Miller, S. A., Custer, W. L., & Nassau, G. (2000). Children's understanding of the necessity of logically necessary truths. *Cognitive Development, 15*, 383–403.

Miller, S. A., Hardin, C. A., & Montgomery, D. E. (2003). Young children's understanding of the conditions for knowledge acquisition. *Journal of Cognition and Development, 4*, 325–356.

Mitchell, P., & Riggs, K. J. (Eds.). (2000), *Children's reasoning and the mind*. Hove, UK: Psychology Press.

Morris, A. K. (2000). Development of logical reasoning: Children's ability to verbally explain the nature of the distinction between logical and nonlogical forms of argument. *Developmental Psychology, 36*, 741–758.

Morris, B. J., & Sloutsky, V. (2001). Children's solutions of logical versus empirical problems: What's missing and what develops? *Cognitive Development, 16*, 907–928.

Moshman, D. (1990). The development of metalogical understanding. In W. F. Overton (Ed.), *Reasoning, necessity, and logic: Developmental perspectives* (pp. 205–225). Hillsdale, NJ: Lawrence Erlbaum Associates Inc.

Moshman, D. (1994). Reason, reasons, and reasoning: A constructivist account of human rationality. *Theory & Psychology, 4*, 245–260.

Moshman, D. (1995). Reasoning as self-constrained thinking. *Human Development, 38*, 53–64.

Moshman, D. (1998). Cognitive development beyond childhood. In W. Damon (Series Ed.) & D. Kuhn & R. Siegler (Vol. Eds.), *Handbook of child psychology: Vol. 2. Cognition, perception, and language* (5th ed., pp. 947–978). New York: Wiley.

Moshman, D. (2004). False moral identity: Self-serving denial in the maintenance of moral self-conceptions. In D. Lapsley & D. Narvaez (Eds.), *Morality, self, and identity* (pp. 83–109). Mahwah, NJ: Lawrence Erlbaum Associates Inc.

Moshman, D. (in press-a). *Adolescent psychological development: Rationality, morality, and identity*, (2nd ed.). Mahwah, NJ: Lawrence Erlbaum Associates Inc.

Moshman, D. (in press-b). Advanced moral development. In T. Wren, A. Tellings, & W. van Haaften (Eds.), *Moral sensibilities III: The adolescent*. Bemmel, Netherlands: Concorde.

Moshman, D., & Franks, B. A. (1986). Development of the concept of inferential validity. *Child Development, 57*, 153–165.

Moshman, D., & Geil, M. (1998). Collaborative reasoning: Evidence for collective rationality. *Thinking & Reasoning, 4*, 231–248.

Nisbett, R. E., Peng, K., Choi, I., & Norenzayan, A. (2001). Culture and systems of thought: Holistic versus analytic cognition. *Psychological Review, 108*, 291–310.

Oliver, P. (1991). 'What do girls know anyway?': Rationality, gender and social control. *Feminism & Psychology, 1*, 339–360.

Orr. D. (1995). On logic and moral voice. *Informal Logic, 17*, 347–363.

Peng, K., & Nisbett, R. E. (1999). Culture, dialectics, and reasoning about contradiction. *American Psychologist, 54*, 741–754.

Piaget, J. (1963). *The origins of intelligence in children.* New York: Norton. [Originally published 1936.]

Piaget, J. (1985). *The equilibration of cognitive structures.* Chicago: University of Chicago Press.

Piaget, J. (1987). *Possibility and necessity.* Minneapolis: University of Minnesota Press.

Piaget, J. (2001). *Studies in reflecting abstraction.* Hove, UK: Psychology Press.

Pieraut-Le Bonniec, G. (1980). *The development of modal reasoning: Genesis of necessity and possibility notions.* New York: Academic Press.

Pillow, B. H. (1999). Children's understanding of inferential knowledge. *Journal of Genetic Psychology, 160*, 419–428.

Pillow, B. H. (2002). Children's and adults' evaluation of the certainty of deductive inferences, inductive inferences, and guesses. *Child Development, 73*, 779–792.

Pillow, B. H., Hill, V., Boyce, A., & Stein, C. (2000). Understanding inference as a source of knowledge: Children's ability to evaluate the certainty of deduction, perception, and guessing. *Developmental Psychology, 36*, 169–179.

Ricco, R. B. (1997). The development of proof construction in middle childhood. *Journal of Experimental Child Psychology, 66*, 279–310.

Ricco, R. B., McCollum, D., & Wang, J. (1997). Children's judgments of certainty and uncertainty on a problem where the possible solutions differ in likelihood. *Journal of Genetic Psychology, 158*, 401–410.

Ruffman, T. (1999). Children's understanding of logical inconsistency. *Child Development, 70*, 872–886.

Scholnick, E. K., & Wing, C. S. (1995). Logic in conversation: Comparative studies of deduction in children and adults. *Cognitive Development, 10*, 319–345.

Siegler, R. S. (1996). *Emerging minds: The process of change in children's thinking.* Oxford: Oxford University Press.

Simoneau, M., & Markovits, H. (2003). Reasoning with premises that are not empirically true: Evidence for the role of inhibition and retrieval. *Developmental Psychology, 39*, 964–975.

Sloman, S. A. (1996). The empirical case for two systems of reasoning. *Psychological Bulletin, 119*, 3–22.

Smith, L. (1993). *Necessary knowledge: Piagetian perspectives on constructivism.* Hillsdale, NJ: Lawrence Erlbaum Associates Inc.

Sodian, B., & Wimmer, H. (1987). Children's understanding of inference as a source of knowledge. *Child Development, 58*, 424–433.

Somerville, S. C., Hadkinson, B. A., & Greenberg, C. (1979). Two levels of inferential behavior in young children. *Child Development, 50*, 119–131.

Stanovich, K. E. (1999). *Who is rational? Studies of individual differences in reasoning.* Mahwah, NJ: Lawrence Erlbaum Associates Inc.

Stanovich, K. E., & West, R. F. (2000). Individual differences in reasoning: Implications for the rationality debate? *Behavioral and Brain Sciences, 23*, 645–665.

Tunmer, W. E., Nesdale, A. R., & Pratt, C. (1983). The development of young children's awareness of logical inconsistencies. *Journal of Experimental Child Psychology*, *36*, 97–108.

Zimmerman, C. (2000). The development of scientific reasoning skills *Developmental Review*, *20*, 99–149.

www.ingramcontent.com/pod-product-compliance
Lightning Source LLC
Chambersburg PA
CBHW050525280326
41932CB00014B/2457

* 9 7 8 1 8 4 1 6 9 9 7 9 0 *